Fanny on Fire

Edith G. Tolchin

"CREATIVE, FUNNY, TOUCHING, AND SEDUCTIVE"

MICHELKIN | PUBLISHING
ROSWELL, NEW MEXICO
BOOKS.MICHELKIN.COM

Other titles from Michelkin Publishing:

Fighting Against Gravity by Rutherford Rankin
The Charming Swindler by Jeff Musillo
Gypsies of New Rochelle by Ivan Jenson
The Ruined Man by Jason DeGray
The Knower by Ilan Herman
Adventures Through the Trees by Kay Gehring
Little Karl by M. Earl Smith & E. A. Santoli
Dear Sun, Dear Moon by Deborah Paggi & Gayle Cole
Irreparable by Jennifer Tucker & Rutherford Rankin

ISBN: 0-9980672-9-6
ISBN-13: 978-0-9980672-9-2
Library of Congress Control Number: 2017914696

"Because if I tell the story, I can make you laugh, and I would rather have you laugh at me than feel sorry for me."

—**Nora Ephron,** *Heartburn*

one

Meet Fanny

Can I help it if I'm just different? I, Fanny Goldman, managed to intercept the Feed Us Channel's protocol. Normally, in order to be a cooking show star on FUC, you'd have to win their Chow-down Competition. Everyone knew that. Sit back, grab a *glazele te* (glass of tea, European-style), and I'll explain what happened...

While I could subsist on watching FUC at odd hours of the day when my menopause-related lack of serotonin got the best of me, a few years ago, in the midst of a wicked night sweat, I found myself planning an attack on the big screen in our bedroom, with the sound turned off. I was silently yelling under my breath so as not to awaken my beloved Solly while my brain bulged almost to the point of bursting.

"Why don't they have any *heimische* (homey) cooking shows on that *ferkokte* (crappy, shitty) channel?" Italian *cucina*: check. French *cuisine*: check. *Cocina mexicana*: check. But not a show in sight featuring *lukshen kugel* (noodle pudding), *gribenes* (crispy bits of chicken skin, fried in chicken fat with onions), or *mandel broit* (sweet loaf cookie)? *Oy vey* (oh my goodness)!

When a brilliant idea—at least one I think is brilliant—enters my mind, if I don't either write it down or act on it immediately, my cannabis-withered brain cells lose it quite quickly. So, at three a.m. I donned the rhinestone-studded purple cat-eye glasses I so desperately need now to be able to take even one footstep without breaking a toe and slipped quietly into our master bathroom. Then, I picked out my perm until I was somewhat presentable and dabbed on my signature red lipstick. I walked into my office across the hall from the master bedroom and recorded a brief YouTube video in which I introduced myself, commented on the network's lineup of international shows, and then ended succinctly by saying, "You need a Jew food show. And I, Fanny Goldman, can cook Jew food."

As soon as I'd finished the short video, I attempted to Google search a contact email that might be connected to a real person at FUC. After only a minute or two, there it was… feedback@feed-us-channel.com. Without any delay, I submitted my rant. But the instant I clicked "send" I realized I was still wearing my damp, hot-flashed purple nightie. *Shit*, I thought. This could only be good if it landed in the hands of someone with a terrific sense of humor, or bad if I became the laughingstock of an entire TV network.

I had pretty much forgotten about this middle-of-the-night communication the next day when the subject line of my email inbox lit up just like my Solly's eyes when he's in the throes of passion, indicating "FUC" as the sender. At first, I thought it was porn spam. But I opened up the message to read it was from someone named Mandiyee Burke. I pictured her as a twenty-something with bleached-blonde hair who couldn't even spell her own first name and probably slept her way to her assistant producer title. The message said simply: *When can you come down to FUC to discuss a Jewish-style cooking show?*

Mameleh (little mother)! Sure, I can cook. Sure, I can write. I've had three books published, countless magazine articles accepted, and a newspaper column printed on a weekly basis. But a TV show? I'm certainly not a celebrity, even if Solly does call me his walking wet dream. More on Solly, the love of my life, later…

Mandiyee made an appointment for me to go down to FUC studios in Chelsea a few days later. *Oy*, I hate *schlepping* into the city. No mass transit for me.

I drove my Nissan Sentra down to the Icon parking lot and gave my keys to the attendant along with a discount coupon. It's not in my genes to pay full price for anything. I walked nostalgically through the neighborhood with which I was quite familiar. It's the same neighborhood where I attended one of the New York City specialized high schools so many years ago.

I reported to FUC's fourteenth floor where I was escorted in royal fashion to a plush, *fency-schmency* peacock-blue room. The blonde Mandiyee—I was right—ordered me to, "Wait here while I call my boss, one of the head producers here at FUC."

I was waiting and checking my Facebook and emails when in walked a tall, dark, and fetching senior movie star type of about sixty-five with a familiar *punim* (face). "Fanny," he said. "Remember me?" In a flash, I was forced to replenish my weed-wilted wits.

Quick, Fanny, think hard. Yes, easy to be hard. This man was most definitely someone I'd *shtupped* (had sex with, or literally, "stuffed"). Wait…1978. I was living at home in the Bronx, but sort of living with that cute and slender David Tobin in his tiny, double-bedded yellow room in a ten-room boarding house in Greenburgh, New York, about a half hour north. David was twenty-two years older; I was twenty-three and he was forty-five. He felt a little unsure of the age difference and encouraged me to date others while still dating him.

The one day that suddenly emerged in my memory was February 14. I had spent the previous weekend with David, and he was driving me home so I could change and get ready for my Valentine's Day trip to the Hotel Hershey with a young Burt Reynolds lookalike. Yes, I had two dates in one day—hell, back then I'd even had three dates in one day. Can I help it if I love my men?

With heavy snow on the roads, David barely maneuvered his 1972 long, yellow Eldorado along the unplowed, slippery streets of the northeast Bronx just in time for me to pack a few bags and change my panties—and yes, I did go braless for the better part of the seventies. I refreshed my red Tangee lipstick and said "Hi" and "Bye" in the same breath to Mommy who must have thought I was employed as a call girl.

Approximately fifteen minutes later, up drove Freddy Giordano in his orange 1975 Datsun hatchback, and we set out, albeit carefully, on our Valentine's trip to Pennsylvania. And Freddy never suspected a thing, even though my heart was racing from the rapid Eldorado to Datsun, hunk to hunk transition.

Wow, do I *ever* remember this guy? The producer in the room was none other than Freddy Giordano, one of the sexiest conquests of my twenties. This Guido Adonis, so many years ago, was a food shop and restaurant inspector for the Westchester County Department of Health. Well, well. Food inspector, food show producer… Same thing, I guess. Who knew?

Time had been kind to Freddy, still with those dark, smiling eyes. His black Italian hair had turned to salt and pepper, as did his mustache which I remember used to tickle the hell out of certain anatomical parts that are not ladylike to mention. He was about to shake my hand when I stood up and instead grabbed him for a huge bear hug.

"Ah, Fanny," he sighed. "I see from the video that you're still wearing those purple nighties."

"I didn't actually *wear* them for long when we were together."

He laughed. Then he asked me, "Do you remember those good times we had together? Let me take you around the studio to meet everyone and see if you can help me convince them about your idea for a Jewish cooking show."

While we were walking through those peacock-colored hallways, I wondered who the hell decorated this place when Freddy said, "If we can convince the network that you're a good fit, I'll adore watching your face on camera. It'll remind me of that night at the Mamaroneck Motel with the whipped cream and cherries." It was *always* about food. "And it will make this old man very happy. Remember Cook's Restaurant in Larchmont, where we always used to go for those early morning-after munchies? I hear it's a bank now..."

As sharp as Freddy still seemed to be, he appeared to have even clearer memories of those events from so many years ago. He was easily distracted from the task at hand: to convince the network that they needed a Jewish cooking show. I have to admit, though: I do remember the erotic food fun at the Mamaroneck Motel.

Freddy called Mandiyee into his office and asked if "The Network Duo" was available. Mandiyee went to check. He said that Myrna Klein and Bobby Fleischman were married and own FUC. Their names did sound Jewish, so I thought maybe that could help me jump to the front of the line. I hoped they were at least not in their twenties because they probably wouldn't appreciate my sense of humor and, of course, my really old recipes. Yet, Freddy called them "the girls" and I began to wonder, why?

After Mandiyee motioned that we should go over to the girls' office, Freddy and I walked down the long corridor to the end of the floor where a bright red door—yes, I said *red*, not peacock blue—had a sign on it that said, "Myrna Klein and Barbra Fleischman," as clear as black and white. We entered to find a couple who appeared to be in their early sixties. Both women stood up as Freddy and I entered the room.

Myrna walked over and, with spindly fingers, shook my hand and said, "I'm Myrna, and I'd like you to meet my wife, Bobby." I walked towards Bobby and she shook my hand with the grip of a Sumo wrestler. Myrna was wearing a tailored red two-piece business suit, with a blazer, pencil skirt, and yes, red stiletto mules. She was tall and had henna-dyed short hair in a beehive style. Bobby, short and squat, wore blue jeans, a man-tailored light blue button-down oxford shirt, black loafers, and, so Myrna wouldn't feel left out (I guess), a red tie. Bobby had thin, dyed black hair with natural wisps of gray, tied back in a ponytail. There's a lid for every pot.

Following the introductions and pleasantries, Myrna, who clearly wore the pants here even though she was wearing a skirt, asked me, "So, Fanny, tell us what dishes you'd like to cook if we create a Jewish cooking show."

I quickly thought of my best dishes and immediately said, "*Brisket with Secret Sauce* and *Matzo Brei with Lox, Onions and Sweet Peppers*. I'll bring you some next time I make them." It was a crapshoot, but *boom*—just like that, I got the job.

Later on, I found out that prior to Freddy's bringing my video to their attention, Myrna and Bobby had been seriously considering adding to their ethnic show lineup. They also really loved brisket and Matzo Brei—as a matter of fact, they loved *any* type of Jewish food since the number of Jewish restaurants in New York City was dwindling. Further, Freddy said they had Google searched me before our meeting to learn about my previous experience with giving engaging speeches and seminars before large crowds and liked what they'd learned so far. Additionally, Myrna told Freddy my YouTube video showed, "That girl has balls."

After I thanked the couple for their decision, Myrna motioned to Freddy to take me back to his office. We all said, "See you soon," and just as the door was closing, I glimpsed at Myrna and Bobby doing a high five, saying, "Yes! *Bubbe's* (Grandma's) cooking. Can't wait!"

Freddy led me down the long corridor back to his peacock blue office and said, "You know they're lesbians, right?" To which I replied, "Duh." I guess he was still a bit stuck in the Jimmy Carter era.

Then we reminisced. He once invited me to live with him in the late seventies in the house he bought in Pleasantville—I couldn't believe it was over thirty-five years ago—but I was otherwise engaged at the time and graciously declined. He's been happily married for thirty years to the same woman, Tina, though they chose not to have children. Of course, I'm about to be married to my Solly. The third time's the charm. And I have two beautiful, grown children. What did you expect, that I'd tell you they were ugly?

So Freddy asked me, "What do we call this show?" Having grown up in Port Chester, New York, in the sixties, Freddy had a lot of Jewish friends and even knew some Yiddish words. Still dumbfounded at this possibility of sudden celebrity, I was at a loss for words, which Solly will tell you is almost impossible.

"How 'bout we call it *Fressing* (Eating) *with Fanny,*" Freddy suggested. I loved his use of "F" words.

I replied with yet another "F" word. "Fabulous!" Apparently, Myrna and Bobby had already given Freddy the green light. All we had to iron out were little details such as format, when to start filming, and, of course, how rich he was going to make me, this ex-lover of mine.

two

Early Fanny

While I was waiting for the rehearsals, I sat in my FUC office-slash-dressing room, and yes, I was able to convince Myrna and Bobby to decorate it in purple, my favorite color. Of course, every time anyone opened the door, the purple would clash with the peacock blue walls in the hall, and even worse when Myrna walked in with her red outfits. But who cares? Purple has always been my color. I even had a purple gown for my senior prom. I'll tell you more about that later.

So, I wait. Boy, am I glad to hear I'll have a teleprompter to read my proposed dialog for each scene because of my PMIIF (post-menopausal insomnia-induced forgetfulness), though Freddy assures me I can improvise a bit. Note to Fanny: what is "a bit"? I figure I should jot down some of my favorite recipes. You never know; although I'm sure I have a bit of an ethnic niche because FUC has never had a Jewish-style cooking show, maybe a little cookbook might help get the word out about Fanny Goldman? Let's see…which recipe should I start with? Fanny, think back…

I've been an outlier from the day I emerged from Jane Goldman's *schnootchkie*

(snatch, vagina). I was valedictorian of the class of 1971 at the prestigious High School of Fashion Industries, though after graduating I never pursued a fashion career. Did making haute couture mini garments for my paper dolls at age seven really provide me with the qualifications to be a fashionista? A borderline genius with an IQ of 140, I was always left with a feeling of being not quite there, which has, in turn, always made me a rebel. I never wanted to follow the rules made by society. Ever.

Oh, and by the way, I skipped third grade in public school in the Bronx because my second grade teacher thought I'd be bored if I didn't go straight to fourth grade. Problem was, within a few years in junior high school, the girls began to sprout boobies, and I, still only ten years old, used up boxes and boxes of Kleenex inside my training bra in a lame attempt to fit in.

Once, a crowd of boys circled me in math class to stare at my chest. Then I realized that the clump of tissues had fallen out of one side of my bra, leaving my left cup flatter than the blackboard to which I was about to be called to solve Mrs. Hoffstein's pre-algebra problem. Snickers were loud as I asked to be excused and zoomed straight for the girls' room to re-stuff, this time with toilet paper. And the following day, that was the end of the training bra until I really needed one about two years later.

Throughout high school, there was Hernando Santiago. Let me tell you how we met. My best friend, Cami, invited me to accompany her to my very first dance at the Pope Pius Catholic High School in the Bronx, where she attended. While my Jewish mother nearly fainted, I threw a tantrum until she finally said, "Go." Daddy was busy napping, or he was just being smart enough to avoid my protests. I guess they realized it was easier for them to surrender than to deal with my outbursts at thirteen.

September 1968: The gym was decorated with tie-dyed signs with peace symbols and black light posters. A cute, short Hispanic boy, José, asked Cami to dance to "My Girl" by The Temptations. This later became their wedding song, though I knew Cami was way too young to get married at nineteen.

With envy, I watched as the crowd of hip kids danced in the middle of the floor. I never imagined I would become one of the cool girls—those who had boyfriends. My confidence was never very strong since I was always chubby. I ate for comfort due to the discord in my home.

The next thing I knew, I felt someone tap my shoulder at the same time a boy in a sharp, olive green sharkskin suit, yellow broadcloth shirt, and matching olive tie, asked me, "Would you like to dance?" Boys, back then, dressed for both classes and dances, neatly in suits. Not like the boys of today whose droopy pants and t-shirts with inappropriate sayings are the norm. Inappropriate for youth perhaps, but not for Fanny. As a matter of fact, I've worn holes in a "Weed & Cock Rock" t-shirt I've owned for the past forty years.

Instinctively, I asked, "Who, me?" I glanced behind me to see if he might be asking anyone else, but no.

He nodded and said, "Yes." I was the one he wanted to dance with.

Hernando Santiago was about five feet, nine inches tall, with dark hair and eyes, and kind of cute if you could get beyond his serious case of acne, which was much like the road map of Texas. I often had to restrain myself from pulling out a marker to play connect the dots.

Here I was only thirteen—though remember, I was hanging out with kids who were always older than I—and the very first time I would dance with a boy, it was to a body-rubbing slow dance. I soon discovered that I liked it. And that dance sealed the deal for "Fanny + Hernando" (heart + heart) for the next three years.

Hernando and I began to go steady almost immediately. Cami told me that the chunky Hillary Hannigan—Hernando had dated her briefly the year prior in ninth grade—often came sniffing around Hernando during classes. It seemed Hernando liked a little meat on the bones, thankfully for me. While Hernando and I were dancing at the following month's Pope Pius dance, Hillary walked up to us and flipped us the peace sign right there on the dance floor. That's when I knew I had to have him all to myself. I never could stand competition.

Hernando was, of course, Catholic, but the difference in religion was never a problem. Hernando seemed fascinated to learn about a new culture (Jewish), and I already knew about his since all of my friends in the northeast Bronx were Catholic. I belonged to one of only two Jewish families on my block. I visited his family during Catholic holidays, and he visited mine during Jewish holidays. And did we both ever reap the benefits of both Puerto Rican and Jewish cooking at their finest.

Hernando was gifted and had an A average at the very reputable Pope Pius. And, of course, I was no slouch in the brains department, though it took me nearly a lifetime to acquire even a smidgen of common sense. So, with my very first boyfriend, I learned that I had a need to be with someone who got even better grades than I; I had an early need to feel challenged. Since we were both in the tenth grade, although I was at Fashion High, we took similar subjects. We'd race home after school and he'd call me to compare grades. Talk about nerds.

Naturally, Hernando was almost two years older than I, even though we were in the same grade. He was born in January 1953 and I was born in November 1954. It was then I discovered that I liked older men. Throughout my life, I have never, ever dated anyone younger.

Hernando was an only child and doted on by his parents. They had him later in life. His dad was a meat packer and his mom a homemaker. The family of three lived in a ground floor apartment in one of the old, but well-maintained apartment buildings with a beautiful stone courtyard facing Pelham Parkway, in the Olinville section of the Bronx. At that time, that area was predominantly Jewish, with a smattering of Puerto Ricans. Wilfredo and Wilma Santiago had moved to the United States just before Hernando was born, and they loved that I spoke to them in fluent Spanish.

We got to see each other almost every weekend whenever Hernando wasn't studying. I did do my schoolwork but hated to study, and personally would have preferred to spend all of my free time with him. However, I understood his priorities, which were not the same as mine, so I just hung out with Cami and my other friends when he was unavailable. That is, when Cami wasn't hanging out with José, the same boy she met at the same dance where I met Hernando. José was from the South Bronx and attended Cardinal Haggarty High School. He was also in the tenth grade. Cami, fifteen at the time, subsequently dated José exclusively throughout high school and they decided to marry at nineteen when they were in their second year at City College where they both majored in accounting.

Their marriage lasted just three short years, and Cami became a young divorcée at twenty-two. They parted amicably, realizing they didn't want to be tied down to the responsibilities of studying, working, and maintaining a relationship at such a young age.

During Easter of 1969, Hernando and I went on a date to New York City to take a walk through Central Park. Of course, back then, I had not yet developed my aversion to the city (any city) and crowds. It was a sky blue spring day and Hernando picked me up at around ten a.m. I wore a navy blue mini-skirt, matching navy blue double-knit vest over a navy blue and white polka dot long-sleeve satin blouse. Always the fashion statement, I had pretty, white, kitten-heeled shoes on my already huge size nine and a half feet, which to me always felt like barges. My feet would plague me all my life. And, after spending just a few hours walking throughout Central Park, I couldn't wait to go home and put my slippers on. But I didn't want to end my date with Hernando, so ouch.

Fortunately, just as I was about to ask to take the subway home, Hernando suggested we go to the movies. We took the subway from Manhattan back to the Bronx, East 233rd Street Station and boy, was I glad we both got a seat. I was thrilled to have Hernando's arm around me for the entire ride on the number two train. We brought the newspaper clipping of the Wakefield Theatre's daily schedule—right, no Internet and no smart phones yet. We settled on the four p.m. showing of *The Prime of Miss Jean Brodie*.

The movie was boring as shit in some parts, so ever the studious, brainiac couple, we decided to examine each other and there began my first make-out session. We were in the back row of sticky, ejaculate-lined seats in the dark Wakefield Theatre, White Plains Road, Bronx. I was fourteen, he was sixteen. What else were we to do? You couldn't play Scrabble in a movie theatre in 1969.

In the summer of '69, while hippies were heading to the Catskills for a love and peace party for 500,000 young folk, Hernando and I would often head to Orchard Beach where I learned what a hard-on was while we were experimenting with each other's bodies on the sand, too old to play doctor.

Seems Hernando was always going to the dermatologist and the doctor gave him a list of foods he shouldn't eat with such a bad case of acne. Chocolate was definitely out—not good for me; I lived on chocolate. Still do. He was such a picky eater. But I guess he couldn't help it with a doctor on his ass like the Soup Nazi. I felt badly for anyone who had dietary limitations even though I was only a teenager. Remember, food has always been my life. Hernando really did enjoy Mommy's chicken soup, though.

Well, Mandiyee will soon be calling me to take a walk down the long peacock corridor to start my rehearsals. While it is easy for me to do my own short, gray-tinged, brown, curly hair, Zsa Zsa—with the purple hair—does my makeup. I found out that Freddy personally selected her for me because of our common favorite color. Before rehearsals, I type a few notes down on my iPad. I've already written two books, so what could be so hard about writing a cookbook? Hmm… that's it: *Grammy Jane's Jewish Penicillin.*

three

Sweet Sixteen+

S o, I've finally gotten through a few days of rehearsals and we're about to go
live. I absolutely love the set because they decorated it to look like a real Jewish
kitchen with little plaques inscribed with Yiddishisms like *Ba Tampte* (Tasty) and
L'chaim (To Life)! They even placed a few deep purple Stars of David on the lilac
and white tiled backdrop, over my two stoves and two ovens. There's a fancy,
modern sink to the right, and a huge stainless steel fridge to the left. Fine gray
granite countertops, several cutting boards, and I'll never *ever* have to clean up.
What more could I want?

I'm wearing my *Fressing with Fanny* apron which, of course, has purple
letters on an ecru canvas background. The stylist gave me a nice gray tunic top,
long enough to cover my chunky hips and thighs, which, by the way, Solly calls
his "dessert," and a pair of matching gray tweed trouser pants. I slip on a pair of
silver blingy flip-flops and I'm ready to go.

"Meet the star of her new show on the Outrage Network, *A Dollar
a Dozen*, Malke Suckadick," I proudly begin. In walks a short, dark-wigged,
orthopedic-shod, modern Orthodox woman of about forty-five, who quickly
corrects her last name: Sukenik. Bear in mind, both FUC and the Outrage
Network—owned by friends of Myrna and Bobby—are cable stations. FUC is

15

known as "the gourmet network for *adults* with sophisticated taste buds," so we weren't cut. I heard Myrna and Bobby laughing, but to play it safe on this, my first show, I add, "I've often been told I have a one-track mind." I proceed to tell everyone about her reality show based on Malke's story of raising twelve children on a budget in a religious, strictly kosher home.

"You all *must* buy this new cookbook, *Mama Malke's Recipes*," I add.

Cut to commercial and then back to the show. We'll soon add the fried onions to the cooked potatoes, to mash and combine. We walk over to the large purple stand mixer and Malke struggles with the attachment, trying to align the opening with the spindle.

I couldn't resist. "What's the matter, Malke, can't you find the hole? I'm sure your husband doesn't have that problem." Malke looks puzzled but finally gets the mixer aligned. Hopefully, they'll be able to cut out the background guffaws.

Malke and I then proceed first to crack and then beat the eggs. This now-infamous recipe, which of course I'll use in my cookbook, is a *Knish Omelet*. Genius.

And while I talk about the name of the dish, I also add, "Malke, by the way you beat those eggs, your hubby must be a happy man. And with twelve kids, he must be some *knish nosher* (Pussy eater—*knish* is a Jewish delicacy, typically filled with mashed potatoes and sometimes fried onions, but is also slang for *pussy*)."

Oy, Fanny. So, where did I leave off?

At sixteen, I graduated as valedictorian of the High School of Fashion Industries' class of 1971. I was accepted at both the Fashion Institute of Technology and New York University. I chose NYU because:

First, I couldn't sew to save my ass. My senior year high school design project was a gorgeous purple and silver brocade prom gown. Yes, I could design and draw, but I had to ask the immigrants' children in my class—most of whom had been sewing at their grandmas' knees in the old country—to finish constructing my gown. Yes, I only got a sixty-seven in sewing class, but all my other grades qualified me for number one at graduation.

Also, my then-boyfriend, Hernando, with whom I went steady all throughout high school, was going to NYU.

Last, but not least, during those hippie times in the early seventies, the only requirement for attending the NYU uptown-Bronx campus program was that you choose a major early on. I chose Spanish. I took the easy way out and took only one English course, which was NYU's sole requirement back in the seventies. So, I filled my sixty-two credits with mostly Spanish courses, a few French and Italian courses, and I maintained a 4.0.

Romance languages just came easy for me. I had been speaking Spanish since I was eleven and lived in the Bronx where most of my friends were Hispanic—not to mention Hernando.

NYU was cool. I became the Spanish-speaking token Jew with a Puerto Rican accent, in El Grito Borinqueño, a social group for Hispanic kids. I smoked my first joint in Victor Rios' dorm room in between Spanish classes when I was sixteen going on seventeen during my freshman year. Remember, I skipped third grade, so I was at least a full year younger than the other freshmen. I went back to class, taught by the illustrious Professor Gómez de la Solara, with my first buzz while attempting to get my brain to translate my thoughts from English to Spanish. Maybe that's why my son Mitchell was predisposed to choose communication sciences and disorders with an emphasis on bilingualism for his doctoral studies which he is now undertaking—and quite well if you ask this Jewish mother—at the University of Illinois at Chicago.

Now, did I mention that Professor Gómez was a victim of polio in Cuba in the thirties and maneuvered his wheelchair into the front of our classroom every day where he stayed put for every class? It wasn't long before I figured out the best methods of cheating on tests, including planting my olive-drab canvas hippie backpack in front of me on the desk, while I sat at an angle diagonally across from him, using small pieces of paper with my notes neatly positioned out of his view but directly within mine. From there, I became a serial cheater where my inch-long fingernails hid advanced Spanish literature notes I delicately etched with a sharp number two pencil.

One would think that with the extensive efforts I took to avoid studying, it would have been easier to just study. But I have always been a firm believer that if you were smart, did your work and homework, and participated in class, then you should not have to study for tests. Yes, I was a *tuchas-lecher* (ass kisser or "licker") and the teachers loved me. That's where cheating as an art form got me my dean's list grades. It was all about the challenge and I was never, ever caught in the act. To this day, I will never take any class—even online—that would not permit open book. But I digress…

While the Hernando Santiago relationship lasted throughout high school, it never made it beyond the first few days at NYU because of the gorgeous gene pool of dark, handsome Hispanic boys belonging to El Grito Borinqueño. They led me to begin to trust my three-year-long suspicions during high school that Hernando just might be gay. Everyone called him "Gaylord" behind his back, which as I look back now, was downright cruel. Years later he became an accomplished pediatrician in the Bronx and did, in fact, get married, but my friends all felt it was a marriage of convenience. This was years before gay was *en vogue*. Why, even my Mitchell and his sweet fiancé, Josh, are, duh, gay. Gay, straight—who gives a shit? Love is love.

My two years at NYU flew by in a pot-induced haze even though I ended up with an impressive 3.9 GPA. I dated quite a few of those handsome boys, one of whom—Manuel Rojas—even *schlepped* (travel or drive but literally, means "to carry") up all the way from Lake Ronkonkoma on Long Island to the Bronx one Saturday during school to take me to a party at his house. We slow-danced all night to an old 45 record by the Stylistics that looped around and around on an old turntable and he made an attempt to nail me in his basement. Of course, this good Jewish girl was still a virgin then (surprise) so I made him drive me all the way back to the Bronx and that was the end of Manny. I guess there was word around the guys that the tokin' token Jew put out—but not this token Jew—at least not yet.

I quit NYU after my sophomore year in 1973 when the uptown Bronx and downtown Washington Square campuses merged, thereby closing the Bronx campus. How could they? I was only eighteen and thought I knew it all. Although I could have completed my degree downtown, I was not about to subway-*schlep* two hours each way—a total of four hours per day (and that's when the trains weren't late). I had better things to do, or so I thought back then. Of course, it didn't help that my then-boyfriend, Rafael Aldana, who just happened to be married *and* had scars from needle tracks on his arms, could not have given a rat's ass if I pursued my *higher* education, at least in the academic sense.

I requested a leave of absence and still have the dean's original confirmation letter to this very day in case I ever decide to go back. But then I'd have to follow rules and probably take courses that I don't want to take because NYU's seventies policy of "no requirements other than your major" no longer exists, I'm sure. Note to self: check this out. This Fanny's been known to bend rules in the past.

Meanwhile, as you know, Camila Arena has been my best friend since seventh grade. Cami had Puerto Rican-born parents and was about five inches shorter than I. Although in the sixties it was trendy for friends to dress alike, as pre-teens we tried wearing outfits that *Monkees* fans wore in *Tiger Beat* magazine, but instead ended up looking like the comic strip characters *Mutt and Jeff.* We grew up together on Maxwell Avenue in the Bronx. She learned about *gefilte fish* (popular Jewish fish dish) and *Pesach* (Passover) from my mom, Jane Goldman, and I learned all about *pernil* (Hispanic pork dish) and *pasteles* (a pork-filled Hispanic delicacy) from her mom, Irma Arena.

Camila, who was studying to be an accountant at City College, had begun working at the Soundview Beach Club in the Bronx for the summer and heard they had openings for additional cashiers when I needed a summer job. When I discovered the *free brisket*, I was hooked. You'll learn later on about the effect brisket really has on me. I just loved to eat; I was *zaftig* (literally, "tasty"—refers to deliciously overweight women) and always had a little meat on my bones which the men seemed to love. And Jimmy the Groper, the ancient, cigar-puffing Jewish cafeteria manager with the thick Bronx accent was the price to pay for the free brisket. Not one girl cashier was exempt from his wandering hands. And back then, in the early seventies, sexual harassment lawsuits initiated by hungry teenagers were a rarity. Grin and bear it, *goily*.

I met ladies' man Rafael Aldana in the cafeteria of Soundview, where I worked as a cashier during the summers of my freshman and sophomore college years. Brisket, corned beef, pastrami, and knishes, among many other kosher-style delicacies, were abundantly dispensed gratis during our lunch breaks and would create in me a lifelong predisposition to Jewish deli *haute cuisine*.

Rafael was visiting the beach club as a guest of a member and approached me with his half-Italian, half-Puerto Rican suave style, a sexy-for-the-time cigarette dangling from his lips, and immediately asked me, "How'd you like to go out sometime?"

He was six feet tall and had long, slicked-down curly brown hair. I was besotted with his bad-boy looks. At seventeen I didn't smoke, but when I graduated from cafeteria cashier to poolside candy stand manager towards the end of the summer, the free cigarettes were too good to pass up, especially now that I had a boyfriend who smoked.

Seemed like everyone smoked back then, even at home. Daddy smoked pipes and cigars and Mommy smoked one Mapleton cigarette every evening which she said helped her relax. Matter of fact, when she died in 2001, we found a twenty-year-old pack in her dresser drawer, still bearing the faint scent of maple syrup and tobacco.

The Rafael thing lasted just the two summers I worked at Soundview and it was a nasty breakup. I decided, at nineteen, that I no longer wanted to go out with a twenty-four-year-old married man who kept on saying he was planning on getting a divorce but couldn't afford it. He was also planning on getting a job. Sure.

I finally decided it just wasn't fun going on a "date" to his mom's apartment in the projects in a dangerous neighborhood in the South Bronx to watch his younger brother shoot heroin in the hall bathroom. While their mom watched *The Price is Right* in the living room, Rafael exhaled pot smoke into his poor dachshund's little snout and then had his way with me in his old bedroom. It was the best of ghetto entertainment.

A year before, Rafael was smart enough to wait until my eighteenth birthday to invite me to his house, then threatened, "If you don't put out, you'll have to take the subway home by yourself." I was no longer jail bait. Back in the early seventies, it would not have been in my best interest as a single girl to take a subway ride from the South Bronx to the East 233rd St. Station alone at night. Happy birthday, Fanny. Your gift is rape.

Birth control? Well, um, no. He had scars all over his upper torso which he said were a result of being struck by lightning as a boy. This, he claimed, rendered him sterile.

By the time I finally got rid of Rafael, I had to beg Daddy for help. When I first started going out with Rafael and my parents clearly disapproved, Daddy said that if I ever needed him to get me out of a tight spot, I should just ask. Daddy was wise and prescient without being overbearing. It was obvious to everyone other than me that Rafael was a hoodlum, but perhaps I just wore blinders for the duration.

After I broke up with him on the phone, our family received many death threats by mail in the form of individual letters cut out of a newspaper and pasted onto a sheet of paper stating, "Your daughter will die for what she did!" We had to get an unlisted phone number and visited the 47th precinct to file a police report. The unlisted number really messed up Daddy's home-based sign painting business for a while until he was able to notify all of his customers, pre-computer age, of the change.

I told you I was an outlier, right?

Now, I've filled you in on my school years and we've shed a few tears. Sit back, have a *shtikel rugelach* (a piece of Jewish cookie), and let me tell you a bit about Mommy and Daddy, more about my adult life, and about my love of food. If you are a good audience, I'll tell you about a few of my *geshmak* (tasty) dishes.

four

Matchmaker, Matchmaker, Not Such a Match

My gorgeous daughter, Lori Feinman, and my brilliant and handsome soon-to-be PhD son, Mitchell Feinman, are coming for a visit next weekend along with their respective fiancés, Paul Lebowski and Joshua Eldred. Seriously, what Jewish mother doesn't say this about her kids?

Apparently, they held a joint summit (read: texted each other) and put in a special request: "Fanny, can you please make us your *Vegetarian Chopped Liver a la Seashore Hotel*?" For some reason, they've always called me by my first name. How can I say no to my kids? Besides, it's not such a hardship to make this dish. It's simply delicious if I say so myself (and by now you know *I will*) but it is also known to be a bit of a love potion since Solly always gets amorous after he eats it. He says it makes him want to eat *me* afterward...

Mommy was a good cook in the old-school style of frying everything and adding *schmaltz* (rendered chicken fat), sugar, or whatever *verboten* (forbidden, prohibited) items have been long since deemed unhealthy by modern dieticians. *Gribenes* (fried chicken fat with onions) was a *Shabbos* (Sabbath) treat for us every Friday night. *Schmaltz* added a little *ta'am* (taste) to boring matzos during Passover.

Jane Baum Goldman was born in New York City in 1919. She, like me, was the youngest of the Baum clan and coincidentally, like me, also had two older brothers. Her early life, however, was quite tragic. When she was seven, her middle brother Benny was ten, and her oldest brother Reuben was about to turn thirteen. Her parents, Minerva and Seth Baum had recently divorced. As Mommy told us the story, poor Reuben never made it to his Bar Mitzvah. He apparently had an undiagnosed heart ailment which took him only a few days before he would become a man according to Jewish tradition.

A short time after that misfortune, Jane's mother, Minerva, died after a 1920s illegal back-room abortion due to unsanitary conditions. Jane and Benny were suddenly up for grabs. Minerva's sister and brother-in-law, Golda and Isaac Worob, lived in Poughkeepsie, New York, which was considered the country in those years. The Worobs were one of the wealthiest families in the town. They owned a dry goods store on Main Street. Little Jane was not permitted to see her daddy, Seth, after the divorce but her brother, Benny, was sent to live with Seth in New Jersey after Minerva's death. Jane, at seven, was taken to be raised, she later told us, as a poor little rich kid in the country with the Worobs.

Jane only saw Benny on rare occasions and never saw her dad, Seth. Back in the twenties, if your mother and father divorced there was no visitation and fathers were blacklisted. That is, at least, as prescribed by Isaac Worob who apparently had little concern for the emotional well-being of his newest dependent.

Thus, little Jane became depressed during the Depression, a mental condition that haunted her throughout her sad life. Her mother was gone and her father was alive, but Jane was never permitted to see him. Lack of maternal—and paternal—love plagued her, rendering her unable to exhibit signs of love, ultimately, towards my daddy, Michael Goldman.

Yes, Jane grew up in relative luxury, but since Aunt Golda and Uncle Isaac Worob had their own two children, Linda and Ian, Jane always felt like a second-class citizen. Linda and Ian went to Ivy League schools, but Jane was not permitted to attend college.

Uncle Isaac told her, "We did enough for you, taking you off the streets and giving you shelter." She certainly had the brains. I remember her doing the *New York Times* Sunday crossword puzzles within a few minutes in ink and *The Daily News Jumble* in under a minute. So, after graduating from Poughkeepsie High School, Jane had the option of working in the family dry goods store on Main Street, getting married, or joining the military since it was war time.

Jane chose the latter and joined the Women's Army Corps (WAC) in 1943. This was her first time away from Poughkeepsie and she found she loved traveling around the South where she was stationed for a few months in Georgia and another few months in Boca Raton, Florida. She served as a secretary, having studied a commercial course during high school. She was a whiz at Gregg Stenography. After six months, she had the option of re-upping when Uncle Isaac begged her to come home. He really missed her (read: her efficiency of managing his store for free room and board with no significant salary). So Jane, torn, returned to Poughkeepsie and took a job building guns at IBM's headquarters to help the war effort while working evenings and weekends at the family dry goods store.

When she was twenty-five and already considered an old maid by forties standards, a match was made for Jane, who by that time was tall and had black hair, dark eyes, and a serious overbite. Aunt Golda and Golda's sister, Aunt Abby, introduced her to a neighbor's son from upper Manhattan. Michael Goldman, who later became my daddy, was a skilled artist and sign painter. Son of Salman and Emma Goldman, Russian immigrants, Michael had hazel eyes, a Semitic nose, and a constant smile. He had an older brother and two younger sisters. Emma Goldman barely spoke English, and when she did, it was with a heavy Russian-Yiddish accent. But could my *Bubbe* (Grandma) cook up a storm! As I've told you, with Jews, it's always about food.

During our Sunday visits when I was little and Daddy was able to drive us between working two jobs, *Bubbe* used to give me Dentyne cinnamon chewing gum, a dessert that was a great complement to her barley-mushroom soup, thick and peppery. And Salman, who owned a newspaper stand until the day he died at the age of seventy-eight in 1966, had a sparkle in his eyes whenever his grandchildren visited, even though he was sleeping most of the day having worked from night to early morning.

Also born in 1919 in New York City, Michael became a sign painter by trade. He studied commercial art and sign lettering during high school in New York City. The matchmaker sisters thought, "Same age, both born in New York City, both Jewish... good enough!" The two subsequently met and the deal was sealed. But was it really good enough?

Jane Baum and Michael Goldman were married on August 5, 1945, in New York City, with a party provided by Golda and Isaac Worob who told Jane, "No one could run our store like you!" Isaac was losing his smart, cheap labor.

Daddy, on the other hand, was never depressed during the Depression. His sunny disposition and engaging sense of humor attracted everyone who crossed his path. Where else did all the Goldman children get their penchant for off-color jokes and *kibbitzing* (telling funny stories)? It was certainly not from Jane who clearly vocalized her negative opinions about her life situations and enveloped visitors in her permanent black cloud. Daddy Michael was her target for misery, a role I later shared with him. As an adult, long after both Jane and Michael were gone, I realized after *years* of therapy, how sad it was for both of them to stay in a relationship of constant bickering and Mommy's anger, which she was never able to reconcile. I vowed never to let that happen to me, and when it did, I made sure to get out and save my sanity.

My two older brothers, Marty and Harold, were the lucky ones. Tall and skinny with dirty-blonde hair, Marty, the oldest, was born in 1947. He was always out and about with his Bronx greaser friends, cavorting in fast sixties cars. Jane couldn't catch him to badmouth him. Harold, slightly shorter, brown-haired, cute, and chunky, was born in 1949. He left the household just a few years after graduating high school to join the Army. It was the Vietnam era of the draft and his number was low; so, by enlisting, he got sent to Heidelberg instead of Hanoi.

I wrote letters to Harry every week so he wouldn't be too homesick, although he was already engaged to Karen and she did the same. Harry once sent me an assortment of French perfumes in petite, bold-colored bottles from the German PX. I was so in love with that gift that I stretched it for ten years by taking one dab at a time from each tiny bottle.

Marty managed to avoid the draft. Our Poughkeepsie cardiologist cousin wrote Marty a convincing letter to take with him to the draft board explaining a rheumatic heart condition. Whether fact or fiction, he got a 4-F classification categorizing him as unfit for service. Marty used to sneak me—when I was just fourteen—into the local clubs in Westchester. We'd listen to his friends' musical group play all the rock standards. Though eighteen was the legal bar age in the late sixties, no one ever questioned me or asked for ID. I grew to love those thick, frothy piña coladas and sweet apricot sours.

I was the youngest sibling still living at home, so I became the emotional pincushion of Jane Goldman. Until I started dating at thirteen (remember, all my friends were a year or two older), I would be witness to Jane's incessant *hocking* (verbal spewing; literally, "hitting") at poor Daddy. I was required to listen to Mommy spew how bad he was for simply wanting to escape to his room to listen to calming Perry Como music at the end of the day after working his two jobs. But if he wanted to engage in civil conversation with Mommy, she wanted no part of it. You're damned if you do and damned if you don't.

Daddy had a sign painting shop in our dark and dank, turpentine-scented, unfinished, tiny cement slab basement. He produced hand-lettered masterpieces for satisfied mom-and-pop stores throughout New York City for almost forty years. In his day job, he was an automotive parts salesman for Sears, Roebuck & Co. in New Rochelle, New York. He did that for twenty-five years, retired in 1984, then up and died in 1987.

Years later, and thousands of dollars in co-pays, therapy was my salvation. I learned that Daddy should have just stood up to Mommy early in the game and told her to "Fuck off; I am not the cause of your misery. Get some counseling." Of course, for the most part, lower middle-class New York Jewish men in the 1950s just accepted their lots and visited the occasional whore in Harlem. Or so my Uncle Sandy, Daddy's older brother, told me when I became an adult. Daddy did seem awfully happy when he came home after his annual vacation "bus trips" with his best friend and fellow Sears employee, Alvin. Jane and Michael never went away on vacations together—they didn't even sleep in the same room.

We did all go away together *once* as a family—all five of us—in the late fifties when I was three, to the kosher Seashore Hotel in Asbury Park, New Jersey. All I remember, even though I was only three years old, is their wonderful Jewish cuisine. Yes, it's always been about food! I also remember Jane preventing herself from enjoying the time away with her husband and children because she just had to find something to complain about. The hotel room was too small. The soup was cold. The pool was too crowded. *Oy.*

Even though I was very young, I recall something we ate at the hotel that tasted similar to Mommy's chopped beef liver but was called *Vegetarian Chopped Liver a la Seashore Hotel*. It was creamy and delicious. As I got older, I made periodic attempts over the years to replicate that recipe, which I finally perfected by the time I had my own children.

Mommy kept a kosher home—that is, until I was ten years old and the nearby kosher butcher closed shop. The neighborhood was changing and the Jews were fleeing the Bronx for the suburbs of Westchester and Long Island. We did eat non-kosher foods outside of the house like many nice Jewish folks did back then. The weekly Sunday Chinese take-out was a treat to be consumed on paper plates because we still had two sets of kosher dishes and silverware for everyday meat and dairy dishes. And, of course, two extra sets of dishes and silverware for Passover dairy and meat. It was quite confusing if you ask me or anyone else in the secular world. "You don't cook the kid (goat) in the mother's milk," has been the biblical belief of observant Jews for thousands of years.

Eventually, after all three Goldman siblings flew the coop, all four sets of dishes got intermingled just like my two older brothers who intermarried. Then we no longer required paper plates on which to eat chicken and other *treyf* (unkosher) meats bought at the local A&P on Baychester and East 233rd. Again, I was the only outlier child who didn't intermingle-slash-intermarry. Although I dated men from just about every ethnic group you can name, each of my husbands has been Jewish.

The only fortunate exemptions from the atmosphere of gloom were, later on, Jane's grandchildren, on whom she doted in her own miserable way. She consistently stuffed them with sweets. For Jane, candy equaled comfort equaled love. Poor Daddy Michael lived with her for forty-one years and escaped the sadness by an early death at the age of sixty-seven due to uncontrolled diabetes, perhaps by choice. Fox's U-Bet chocolate syrup was a staple in the Goldman household for Daddy's daily egg creams, which were toxic for diabetics. Years later, I tried to make sense of their relationship: Jane claimed she hated Michael, so why did she overindulge him with sweets?

five

Togi America

As predicted, Solly was quite thrilled with last night's *Vegetarian Chopped Liver a la Seashore Hotel*, which literally kept him *up* until the wee hours. Although I'm fairly tired this morning, do you think I'm going to *kvetch* (complain) about having a man in his mid-sixties with a very active, um, libido? Note to self: I must Google search all of the ingredients to see which, among the green beans, butter, onions, hard-boiled eggs, spices, and walnuts, might be the aphrodisiac.

I'm resting my sore *tuchas* (ass, butt, tushy)—thanks, Solly—on a thickly-cushioned purple vinyl-topped stool on the side of the set and going over the three recipes of the day with Mandiyee, who then sets the interns out shopping the Chelsea Market for the ingredients. When they return, Puff and Duni-B, the interns I'll talk about a little later on, begin to prep them. I've grown to like Mandiyee; I guess she's not the dumb blonde I thought she was, even if she is a *shikse* (not Jewish, or Gentile female). And another recipe I know for sure I'll use in my cookbook—although Freddy doesn't even know about *that* yet—is my *Not Sushi Tuna with Avocado and Lemon*. Simply scrumptious, and reminds me of the time I worked for a Japanese fish importing company…

Although I was still living at home in the Bronx after I left NYU, it was about time I started earning some money to support my Jewish Princess tendencies. Mommy and Daddy were fairly poor and my leaving school at nineteen with no career in sight did not help matters any. So what did smart girls do back in 1973? Most of us went to Carly-Girl Employment Agency in Midtown Manhattan to see what types of jobs were available. I took the express bus from the stop in front of the Chicken Delight—a frequent fattening *nosh* (snack)—at East 233rd Street and White Plains Road, directly to a tall, nondescript beige building in Midtown Manhattan.

I had stopped taking the subway at age sixteen after I was mugged during a particularly violent race riot on the number two train as it was passing, northbound, through the South Bronx. This scared the living crap out of me, especially when a young thug stole my watch right off my wrist and then commenced to touching my thigh. Luckily, we had reached the next station and an interesting old character entered as the doors opened. The hoods ran over to him and punched the poor old man in the face, blood splattering everywhere. I ran to the first car to wait by the conductor until the ruckus died down with the arrival of the NYPD.

Of course, the express bus took much longer because I was at the mercy of the traffic above-ground, whereas being underground, after that incident, caused me high anxiety that I never really overcame.

Anyway, I walked through the marble hallway and approached the elevators. The elevator operator took one look at me and simultaneously stated and asked, "Carly-Girl, eighteenth floor, right?" What, was I wearing a sign that said: "Unemployed Jewish Princess Going Through Job-hunting Motions Until She Finds a Husband"?

While I was in the waiting area, Larry Bushman (what a name, right? And he *did* look like a man who liked the bush), called me into his office. His first question was, "Can you type?" He never bothered to discuss my education, or even to ask for a résumé. Didn't matter, I didn't have either. Since I did pass seventh grade typing (even though it was almost ten years earlier), I nodded yes.

"Good," Mr. Bushman said. "Report tomorrow morning at nine a.m. to Togi America Import-Export on 16 East 40th. Ask for Yuki." For some reason, I didn't even need a formal interview, but I soon learned why they wanted young American gals—and why they couldn't keep them.

Yuki, the office manager, was a short, subservient, middle-aged Japanese woman with a serious spine curvature. She giggled in a high-pitched tone. She was the only Japanese woman in the office. Matter of fact, the open floor plan consisted of about twenty Japanese men, and each had his own very young American female assistant, though we were called "clerk typists" and "secretaries" back then.

There really wasn't much for me to do as I had never really worked in an office before. It appeared that the business was very successful as the men were always on the phone and talking to each other in Japanese. While I waited to be assigned something, I brought my book, *E-Z Typing: 1-2-3*, and practiced on the new IBM Selectric with self-correcting key, which I repeatedly used to delete my frequent errors until my practice made progress.

At this point, I had never heard of the term "import-export," so all I knew from Mary, the tall, eighteen-year-old blonde receptionist, was that they imported frozen fish and a famous brand of bicycles from Japan. The first thought I had was, "Oh good. Maybe I'll get some free *gefilte fish* here." Clearly, again, it was always about food, even though I knew nothing about sushi and rock lobster tails at the time, which was actually what Togi America imported. But what I also learned was that most of the young American ladies who worked at Togi were having affairs with the Japanese married male executives.

Sara Ornstein, a tall, attractive, slender, dark-haired Jewish girl from the Pelham Parkway section of the Bronx, introduced herself after a few days and we hit it off immediately. No affairs for Sara; she had an Orthodox Jewish upbringing and her parents kept kosher at home. At lunch, she would tell me about who was doing whom and how Mary the receptionist was "dating" the quite married young Mr. Oshiro whose wife had just had a baby.

Sara's boss was a middle-aged, happily married family man (a rarity in *this* office), named Mr. Nakata. When he got excited, he had a tendency to speak in Yiddish due to his many years of trading fish with Hasidic Mr. Silverstein, his best customer. Mr. Nakata invited Sara and me to lunch at the Playboy Club at 5 East 59th Street. How glamorous was it for a nineteen-year-old gal from the Bronx to walk through a restaurant where celebrities dined and bunnies hopped from table to table?

Mr. Nakata took the liberty of ordering for us. When the sushi arrived, the bunny-slash-server placed the elegant plates on the white linen-topped table. After one bite, the first words out of my mouth were, "Bleccch. This doesn't taste like *gefilte fish* to me. It doesn't even taste like my special recipe tuna salad." You can take the girl out of the Bronx… Fortunately, Mr. Nakata had a good sense of humor and certainly knew from his Jewish customers that *gefilte fish* was *cooked* and sushi, not yet popular in the early seventies, was in fact *raw*. And I never ate anything raw, still don't, even now. My prime rib has to be cremated. Thankfully, he ordered me a well-done beef dish while Sara laughed throughout the entire lunch.

After a few weeks, I was assigned to be the "office girl" to the ancient Mr. Nishimura who routinely fell asleep at his desk after lunch. No one ever said anything to him because he had apparently been with Togi America for over thirty years and the Asian co-workers were very respectful of age. One afternoon, at around three p.m., Mr. Nishimura awoke with a startle and proceeded to remove his shoes and socks at his desk, smack in the middle of the very large un-cubicled office. My desk was right next to his and I began to think he was stripping naked. But I was wrong. He then grabbed a toenail clipper from his center desk drawer, looked at me quite seriously in his bare feet, and asked, "You crip toenails?"

Outraged, I looked at the old guy straight in the eyes and muttered, "*Putz nosher* ("cocksucker")," loud enough for Sara's Yiddish-speaking boss, and Sara who also spoke fluent Yiddish, to hear across the room. I quit on the spot. This was the peak of the feminist movement. Throughout my years of being employed by others, one thing I made a point of never doing was preparing coffee for male supervisors, required of all seventies and eighties female office workers. Add to that BBJs (boss blowjobs) and clipping one's manager's toenails.

I walked down the center aisle of the office to open mouths and shocked stares and signaled to Sara, "See you later." I said goodbye to Mary as I walked out past the reception area into the elevator, wishing I had stolen one of the famous bicycles in the adjacent showroom.

Looking back so many years ago, I realize Mr. Nishimura was raised in a society where a woman tended to men's grooming habits in the old country. He had never learned that that practice just didn't transfer culturally when he moved to the United States. It was then I learned that being submissive, for me, was just plain *tsuris* (trouble).

Back to Carly-Girl Employment Services, *again*.

Myrna and Bobby joint-texted me, IN CAPS (they were excited), to let me know that next week, we'd have Penny the Pole Dancer on my show. Who the hell is Penny the Pole Dancer? Note to self: Google search her tonight…

six

Penny and Simon

Puff and Duni-B, interns *extraordinaires*, are busy on the set, prepping the ingredients and getting the two slow cookers ready. One slow cooker is for the demo, the other is actually in operation during the segment. Now, Puff is known to do just that—puff—before work, after work, and sometimes during breaks. No one cares; she does her work well and is always happy. Though she is only in her early twenties, she looks like a tall, slim, matured dandelion whose top has turned into a puffball, with her white, ball-shaped Afro—a sharp contrast to her smooth, African-American dark bronze skin tone.

Duni-B is short, Hispanic, and when asked about her unusual name, states, "Do you live in a cave? My mom always loved Dooney & Bourke bags and accessories. Can't you tell?" as she shakes her upper extremities. All you see hanging from her little fat wrists, up and down her lower arms, are the D&B-logoed bangles. Personally, I love the way those gals interact while they are working—especially when Duni-B curses at Puff in Spanish behind her back.

Today, I whispered back to Duni-B, "*Te oigo* (I hear you)," and she was shocked that this Jew spoke and understood *her* language. And Puff sometimes calls Duni-B "Doobie."

About a half hour later, the colorful interns have finished their chores

37

and the set is ready. Lighting is being checked as Zsa-Zsa tweaks my makeup, though this Fanny ain't too shabby for sixty.

"My culinary partners in crime, I'd like you to meet Penny *Pisher* (pisser, one who urinates)." Giggles. "Oops, sorry. I mean Penny (Penina) Pinsker, author of a new cookbook with foods from her native land, Israel. Penny's book is called *From Pole to Plate.*" Chuckles.

"Today's dish is *Cholent* (a slow-cooker stew), a dish that contains everything but the kitchen sink. Normally it would be cooked in a low-heated oven overnight on *Shabbos* (the Jewish Sabbath) by Orthodox Jews who, by religious law, are not permitted to turn an oven on and off. But by the magic of TV and an excellent slow-cooker, we'll be preparing it right now. Penny, tell us about the ingredients…"

"Chunks of beef stew meat, lots of beans, potatoes, onions, and barley make up the dish." This *sabra* (Hebrew for native Israeli) is just exquisite. She's about thirty-five, with long, shiny black hair and a body like I used to have in my twenties. One that made men howl in the dark. Or was that the dogs mating in the Bronx back alley? I'm loving listening to her trill her Rs. "Barrrrley." She reminds me of Simon Dubinsky whom I'll tell you about in just a bit. The food is done and plated and we eat this seasoned, old school Jewish comfort food with gusto.

"So, Penny, what exactly is pole dancing?" Wow, I really must get out more. Penny just laughs as Doobie—sorry, Duni-B, opens up the lavender canvas curtain on the other side of the set to reveal two shiny poles the likes of which I haven't seen since I took the number two IRT Line from the Bronx to Manhattan many years ago. They look exactly like those sleazy, bacteria-ridden floor-to-ceiling subway poles that dirty old men in raincoats used to latch on to in crowded cars only during rush hour, while they proudly worked the false pockets in their raincoats to reveal their manhood. Ewww. Fortunately, these two poles were shiny and clean.

"What's next?" I ask Penny.

She says, "I have a surprise for you." She takes me by my hand over to the poles. She then positions me next to my pole, takes hold of hers, and begins to show me her moves. Fortunately, I'm wearing comfy, soft, stretch-waist navy velour knit sweatpants and a royal blue velour sweatshirt with navy-bejeweled flip-flops, of course.

Just as we both start swaying, Penny says I'm a natural. I quip, "Actually, I've been dancing on Solly's pole for a long time now." By the fifth time around the poles, the beans in the *cholent* start to do their job and both of us begin to pass gas quite robustly. Straight-faced, I look right at Penny and add, "Ahhh. With this recipe, I can finally kiss the Metamucil goodbye."

Israelis—that brings me back to Simon Dubinsky, to whom I was engaged from 1974-1977…

Actually, Simon had been dating, or should I say, *doing*, Arlene Gladstein all throughout high school. I knew Arlene through Cami; they had met each other as toddlers when they both lived in the South Bronx. Arlene was then living off of the Grand Concourse in a pre-war, seven-story building with cockroaches in the bathroom so large I had to dodge them in order to sit on the toilet. First time I had ever seen them.

One day, while I was visiting Arlene during *Pesach* (Passover), she told me how she didn't trust Simon even though they had been involved in a sexual relationship from the time she was sixteen through nineteen. Red flag number one for Simon Dubinsky. To drown her sorrows, she proceeded to down an entire box of Streit's chocolate-covered Passover macaroons while I watched. When she got to the last one, she looked at me, with mouth full, and asked if I'd like the last one.

Poor Arlene was obese. Neither of her sisters, Miriam and Molly, lived to thirty as they literally exploded from overeating. Years later, Cami heard from our old circle of Bronx friends that Arlene never made it to fifty.

Arlene said she was about to break up with Simon but she was too proud to realize their relationship was just sexual. Arlene had clues Simon was frequenting a house of ill repute in Tijuana during his leaves from the naval station in San Diego. That day I was visiting with Arlene, Simon happened to pass by as he was seeing friends in a nearby apartment building. I was getting ready to leave and take the cross-town bus home to the Northeast Bronx, when Simon said, "Good, I'll take the ride with you!" I'd always thought he was cute.

We got on the bus, fed our tokens into the machine (yes, this was the early seventies and the MetroCard hadn't been invented yet), and sat down in the back of the bus. All of a sudden, the air began to fill with pheromones along with the pre-DEP exhaust fumes and this nineteen-year-old girl and that twenty-one-year-old fine specimen of a Semite started making out right in front of the disgusted rush hour commuters. When we came up for air, I mentioned the nasty breakup with Rafael and how he threatened my family. Simon immediately assured me, "You won't have to worry now; he'll never come near you or your family again!" Well, I guess this Bronx girly was hooked.

Simon Dubinsky, with light brown hair and a hairy chest (my weakness), was a gorgeous Jewish boy born in Israel in 1952. His parents came to the United States when he was eight years old. Although he had virtually no accent, when he was hanging around anyone in his family who spoke Hebrew, he was prone to trilling his Rs, which sort of sounded like sexy French. I found it quite endearing. His mom also made a mean *cholent*.

Simon and his parents now lived in Teaneck, New Jersey, having moved from the Grand Concourse area in the early seventies when drugs and gangs settled in and Jews began their mass exodus to the suburbs and Miami Beach and Boca. This was the Vietnam era and, like my brother Harold, Simon's number was low. He enlisted in the Navy in 1972, a year after high school graduation. Simon had a challenge learning English and lost a year in school when he was eight, so he graduated high school at nineteen the same year as Arlene and me—in 1971—though we were both sixteen. (Even though she hadn't skipped third grade like I did, Arlene had been in the two-year SPs—special progress classes unique to New York City schools—where in junior high, smart kids would jump from seventh grade to ninth grade).

Simon was now stationed in San Diego. We were dating exclusively, I liked to believe, and writing daily letters to each other until his next leave brought him home. Of course, Arlene was no longer my friend because she could never get him to commit, much less propose.

While I waited for each visit, I brushed up on my Hebrew since I only attended Hebrew school up until I was about ten years old. After that, as my brother, Harold, was already fifteen, post-confirmation, and Martin was almost eighteen and *way* post-confirmation—and back then it wasn't quite as important for a Jewish daughter to go the bat mitzvah route as it was for a Jewish son—our family stopped all religious training. It was too costly for my parents as they belonged to a fairly opulent (by sixties standards) Reform congregation in the Fleetwood section of Mount Vernon, New York. But even back then, I enjoyed learning languages.

So, I read my old Hebrew books and occasionally spoke with Simon, who called from San Diego whenever he had a pocketful of change; though often he would call collect, and Mommy would have a shit fit when the phone bill came in. He used to make me laugh when he told me of his escapades in Tijuana on leave, watching as the prostitutes serviced the donkeys at the local peep shows. I was at once shocked and amused. Fidelity red flag number two.

Simon would write back in third-grade Hebrew script, but when I could not understand I would phone his mom, Sheyna Dubinsky, and ask her what he was saying. Once I got caught because he wrote, "I really want to fuck you when I see you." Fortunately, Sheyna had a good sense of humor and was fairly modern in her beliefs. Sheyna and Leibel Dubinsky had met as teens in Hungary, but both were able to escape the Holocaust by moving to Israel (then Palestine) during the war, and waited to have Simon, their only child, in 1952.

After that pheromone-filled bus ride home from Arlene's, on his next leave, Simon asked me to marry him. So, in 1974, he at twenty-one, and

I at nineteen, became engaged. We went to a jeweler in Pelham, New York, recommended by my brother, Marty, who was already married to Wanda. I was excited to get a ¾-carat heart-shaped solitaire platinum diamond ring and Sheyna arranged an elaborate engagement party for both the Goldman and Dubinsky families, for her only son and his fiancée.

Simon returned to his naval duties in San Diego and we corresponded by phone and daily love letters until he received his honorable discharge at the end of 1975. Simon moved back with his parents in Teaneck and looked for work. Although his dad, Leibel, tried hard to get Simon jobs in construction (which was Leibel's trade), unfortunately, Simon was just not cut out for this line of work. He took a few courses in heating and air conditioning on the GI bill but never made it to the end of classes. Either it didn't interest him, or this also was not the type of work for him. Or he had undiagnosed ADD.

Since he would soon be a married man, he would have to find some sort of work. In the seventies, I was employed as a secretary, administrative assistant, or clerk typist—always in importing or exporting various commodities, whether frozen fish, chemicals or cashews. But in those days, the husband would be the breadwinner since ultimately the wife would be staying home to take care of the children.

This did not bode well because in the three years we were together, Simon held about seven different jobs, each for short periods of time. Red flag number three. While he was a hot number, I soon learned that two bodies grinding together did not always create a perfect environment for a lasting relationship.

In early 1977, I decided to go to one of the local diet doctors, who back then were known to prescribe copious amounts of now-dangerous Tenuate Dospan. I decided that even with a pretty face, I wanted to lose some weight and make a change in my life. In a few months, I lost fifty pounds and went down from a size sixteen to a size seven. All of a sudden, I was getting stares from guys on the street, whereas it only used to be from a select few who liked *zaftig* girls. It was time to become a kid in the big-boy candy store at twenty-two.

Thankfully, I realized that Simon and I were not meant to be together. As I look back, I realize what I did was cowardly, but I had no experience in breaking off an engagement, so I did the best I could. I called Simon and broke the news to him. Rather than keep the ring, I took the high road and told him to come and pick it up. The next evening, he came over wanting to try to convince me to change my mind, but I told my parents to say I wasn't home, even though I was upstairs in my small bedroom I shared with Mommy. He got back the ring and gave Mommy the 14-karat gold tiger ring I had custom made for him as an engagement gift three years prior. That was the end of Simon, or so I thought.

I'm taking a break between scenes in FUC's cafeteria where I'm enjoying the gourmet food. Hello—it's a food channel after all, and all of our top chefs have contributed dishes. Today's special is taco salad with spicy ground beef. I'm indexing the recipes for the book that I'll soon be proposing to Freddy when I remember my first go-to dish, a ground-beef goody that I call *Fanny's Yum-mush*. This, in turn, reminds me of my first *true* love, David Tobin...

seven

Intro by Camera and David Tobin, Part One

O*y*, so many men. At this age, I'm lucky if I can remember all of their names. Freddy walks by my office for a chat and sees me deep in thought. "A penny for your thoughts," he says.

I just smile and say, "It'll cost you a lot more than that."

I tell him I'm just having a déjà vu of the summer of 1977 and he asks if he can sit with me while I reminisce. Well, I never *used to* say no to Freddy.

"By the way, we have a network meeting scheduled for tomorrow at 3:15 p.m.," says Freddy. "Be there or be square."

My negativity kicks in and I start to worry. "Jeez, I hope they're not firing me because of my big mouth," I blurt out, not known for my ability to filter (duh).

Freddy just smiles and says, "It's a surprise."

So, after the Simon thing, this size seven Fanny decided to try a newfangled dating service. It was called Intro by Camera and was located in a plush, dark, and modern shag-carpeted office inside the tall former Sears building in White Plains, New York. Interviewed introductions were recorded on the new-for-1977 VCR technology using VHS tapes. Men would review tapes of eligible ladies as they were prompted with questions by the owner, Mack Sabatino, behind the camera; and of course, ladies would review men's tapes. Same-sex couples, unfortunately, were not part of this service back then, even though Mack would have made a fortune if he had added that option.

I paid the initial $125 for a one-year membership—a lot of money back then—and was videotaped in black and white, though just after I joined the service I found out subsequent recordings were done in color. I ultimately became a lifetime member for $100 more, though Mack refused to re-tape me, merely saying, "You're gorgeous just as you are in black and white or in color." What a salesman. No matter, by my next visit to White Plains, a half-hour drive from the Bronx, I was up and running with a list of guys who had viewed my tape. The rules were, of course, that I had to view and approve their tapes as well and Mack would fill me in a bit about their lives—at least enough to make the connection. No background checks were necessary in 1977.

The Son of Sam Summer of '77... I was a walking basket case before every date I met through Intro by Camera. David Berkowitz, a not-so-nice Jewish boy, stalked and murdered Bronx girls with long brown hair. I was a Bronx girl with long brown hair. For a few months, I would run out to meet my dates in their cars while wearing a kerchief tied under my chin to conceal my hair. My dates understood because Berkowitz was all over the papers.

Through Intro by Camera, I once had dates with both The Fonz's and Ralph Malph's cousins (though not at the same time). Neither meeting was to develop into a relationship because they both lived in Brooklyn and it was too far to *schlep* by car to the Bronx during the late-seventies gas crunch.

Cami had recently become divorced from José but remained friendly with his mom and dad who returned from New York to retire in Puerto Rico, their native country. Cami invited me to go with her to Puerto Rico, my very first trip on a plane at twenty-two. This would be a great way to escape the fear of the city during the summer of '77. Lola and Nando really adored Cami. They welcomed both of us as we landed and drove us to their little, pink, one-story adobe home in the suburbs of San Juan. Lola took us to Luquillo Beach where I wore my sexy black jersey X-shaped (and X-rated) combo bikini-tank swimsuit. Ask me for a picture but cover your eyes.

Cami and I were sunning away when two gorgeous European-looking men approached us and asked, in Spanish, if we wanted to take a swim. As we walked to the water, Cami whispered, "I want the cute one." But since they were both dark and cute, it didn't matter to me.

Well, I got the cute one whose name was Jesús Gonzalez. Cami got Antonio "Tony" Perez who quite frankly looked just like Pancho Villa. Both were pilots from Madrid and worked for Iberia Airlines. They were on an R&R stop in Puerto Rico. We asked no questions about their marital status as they were clearly in their mid to late thirties. And who cared? I was wise enough to know that long, long-distance relationships would not work. We learned that they came to New York frequently. Jesús kissed me right there as the warm ocean water made waves on our floating bodies. Cami was having fun but just didn't have the same attraction to Tony. Plus, she was a lot more reserved than I ever was. Lola, the ex-mother-in-law, seemed amused just watching all of us flirt on the beach.

The studs invited us to meet them at the disco at the El San Juan later that evening. Nando let us borrow his car, and off we went dressed in our skimpy sundresses and sandals. As the valet parking attendant took our keys, Spanish Jesús greeted me with a French kiss and Tony smiled at Cami. We had piña coladas and danced all night.

As the attendant brought the car, Jesús internally tickled my throat while we said goodnight. He promised to call me when he next came to New York. At twenty-two, that was the highlight of my trip to Puerto Rico when it should have been all of the wonderful sightseeing we did, the *comida sabrosa* (delicious food) we enjoyed, and the great hospitality offered to us by Lola and Nando. Skewed and *screwed* priorities would haunt me a good part of my life.

Of course, Jesús did call about a week after I returned to the Bronx and

I drove my gas-guzzling brown 1973 Dodge Dart Swinger, spurting its way down the FDR, to the Biltmore Hotel in Midtown. I spent the night with Jesús on the tenth floor doing things I had never done, Spanish-style. In pre-AIDS 1977 an IUD was certainly sufficient.

Meanwhile, I had a list of eligible men whom I had selected from Intro by Camera. During the previous three or four weeks, some had already watched my tape, some had yet to come in, and one, in particular, had seen it and was intrigued but afraid to contact me. Mack had some selling, uh, convincing to do for one specific man.

Mommy said that someone called while I was away, but didn't leave a message, saying instead that he'd call back. I reviewed my list and phoned Mack to see if anyone had recently come in and approved my tape. He said yes.

In 1977, it was still unheard of for a gal to call a guy first. But, I rationalized, this guy had visited Intro by Camera a few weeks ago and did, *sort of,* approve. I later found out he offered much resistance, but we'll get into that. I took the paper with his number and dialed the phone. I asked for David Tobin but he wasn't there so I left a message. A week went by, and since what I remembered from his tape was favorable—dark hair, Jewish, mustache, tall, IBM programmer, and thirty-five (which was my upper limit since I was twenty-two), I called again. This time he picked up and seemed surprised at my persistence. We made a date to meet a week later.

August 16, 1977—the day Elvis died. The Son of Sam had been apprehended a few days before. David Tobin drove up to my house in the Bronx in his big yellow Caddy (a plus for a girl my age) looking tall, thin, adorable, and sexy. Well preserved for thirty-five, I thought. Off we went for dinner and the only thing I can remember is that we spoke about Elvis and that I was immediately smitten with David's intelligence, smooth talk, brown eyes, and the way he opened the car door for me. He wore a flowered polyester button-down shirt with the first three buttons open to reveal—yes—a hairy chest. Maroon double-knit slacks (a rage in the seventies) and black low dress boots completed his look. He was a sharp dresser, straight out of *Saturday Night Fever.*

After a few dates, we went away for Labor Day weekend at the Quality Inn, Hawthorne, New York. After a night of intense passion followed by a "Don't ever leave me" from David's beautiful Jewish mouth just as he was about to, um, well, you know, he invited me to accompany him to take his son, who was turning eight on Labor Day, to the Bronx Zoo. Little Scott was a sweet redhead, full of energy, and a genius who could do multiplications of three or four figures in his head. It later served him well when he received his Master of Engineering degree from Princeton and went on to earn millions in the financial industry in New York City.

After Labor Day weekend, during a phone call, I told David that he really looked great for thirty-five (as Mack Sabatino had indicated). David asked, "Who said I'm thirty-five?" I told him about Mack and his hard sell tactics. David just said, "I'm actually forty-four." I almost fainted. Twenty-two years older than I? There was no way he looked it. That was the reason why David never returned my first call. He was concerned about the age difference; however, after we met and fell in love—so quickly and so naturally—he stopped worrying, at least for a few years.

But for now, I would have to convince Mommy and Daddy as I was still living at home. We arranged for David to meet them even though Mommy didn't like house guests since her depression prevented her from keeping a tidy home. She was a hoarder.

David spilled the beans in under a minute. They just rolled their eyes and Mommy said to me, "Are *you* sure you're okay with this?" Apparently, I was worried for nothing because my parents were so used to my antics. Whew.

I was in between clerical (and yes, always import-export) jobs while collecting unemployment insurance, so I was free to stay with David. I would check in with the local agency, as needed, to report job interviews (which were a very low priority since living was inexpensive back then) and then drive up to Greenburgh evenings to greet David and make dinner for him.

We'd run to the local A&P to buy ground beef, spaghetti, onions, and ketchup. This was all I could cook with my still rudimentary culinary skills. I would dice the onions and brown them with the ground beef using the rooming house's shared frying pan. I'd add a little salt, pepper, garlic powder, and ketchup to the natural gravy. After boiling the pot of spaghetti, I'd strain it and pour the delicious mush mixture over it. It was perfectly satisfying for my not-yet-foodie-developed taste buds and David was just grateful he didn't have to cook. With the metabolism of youth, I was still able to eat carbs without worrying about them causing gas or settling on my sweet, young *tuchas*.

There were many overnight visits to David's ten-room, ancient, three-story stone boarding house in Greenburgh, New York. David's landlord eventually reminded him about his lease being written for only *one* inhabitant.

During those days of back and forth from the Bronx to Greenburgh, David began to speak about his concern for our age difference. "Twenty-two years might not seem like a lot now, Fanny. But one day it will." And he was right, and we'll get into that *much* later on.

But then I wanted no part of *that* conversation since I loved being with David and I also loved *not* being amid the chaos and dysfunction at the homestead in the Bronx. David mentioned it might be a good idea for me to go back to Intro by Camera and try to meet someone closer to my own age, though we should still date each other and keep in touch because he did love me. Cake and eat it too?

So, that's how I met Freddy Giordano. However, after several dates with Freddy, David began to feel ambivalent about my being with other men, especially when he had to rush me home that Valentine's Day weekend in the blizzard just so I could go away with Freddy.

When Freddy bought a house in Pleasantville and asked me to move in with him, David finally said, "I can't take it anymore. I thought it would be in your best interest to date younger guys, but I love you. Let's get a place together."

Thursday, 3:15 p.m.:

Mandiyee is setting up the conference room and motions for me to sit on the right side in the center of the long, black, iron table. Yes, the room is peacock blue (Freddy's idea). If it were up to Myrna and Bobby, of course, it would be red. Water bottles are set out, along with a few plates of maple leaf cookies courtesy of Cody Banks, the Canadian chef and star of FUC's hit show, *From Canada with Love.* I never thought anyone in Canada knew how to cook.

Bobby walks in first, dressed in a plaid flannel shirt, jeans, and standard black loafers—no red tie today, but a red scrunchie on her now-braided ponytail, and her arm around Myrna's waist. Such a loving couple. Myrna's wearing another tailored red suit—this time pants—and her red suede mules. Bobby holds the chair for Myrna as she sits down at the head of the table with Bobby to her immediate left. "Thanks, Babe," says Myrna.

Freddy comes in and sits at the opposite end of the table, facing Myrna, with Mandiyee to his left. Puff and Duni-B and a few other assistants stroll in and the meeting begins at 3:15 p.m. promptly. Freddy is smiling like he used to, over thirty-five years ago, every time we'd exit the Mamaroneck Motel.

Oh shit. My heart is racing. They'll surely fire me.

Myrna opens the meeting by thanking everyone for attending. Puff and Duni-B are texting away on their phones and I see Puff's screen showing: *This is fucking boring.*

On the big screen in the center of the large windows facing Chelsea, they're playing my segment with Malke Sukenik and the *Knish Omelet.*

When I'm nervous, I blurt. So, here goes. "Okay, before you let me go, I want to apologize for fucking up so badly and wasting your time." Myrna, Bobby, and Freddy looked at me, one more startled than the other.

Bobby, who never says anything if Myrna is around, interrupted me with, "Stop, Fanny. You're amazing." I guess she really has balls after all.

Myrna takes over, straight-faced, with, "We've just received word that *Fressing with Fanny* is a runaway hit. There's talk our show might come up for a

SAMMY award, which, as you all know, is short for 'sandwich' and is daytime food TV's equivalent of the Emmy award."

Then she smiles (finally…I've never seen Myrna smile before) and adds, "I don't know how you do it but keep it up and make sure you come up with a bunch more of those amazing recipes." Wow. "Bobby and I haven't eaten this well since our *bubbes* were neighbors in Brooklyn."

Freddy, strutting (in his seat) like a proud peacock—now I see it's his favorite color for a reason—shouts out, *"Mazel tov* (Congratulations! Literally, good luck!), Fanny," in his best New York Guido Yiddish.

I didn't know whether to cry or laugh, but for sure I was about to wet my pants from relief. Is this a dream? Of course, still unable to contain myself, I offer, "Well, I hope everyone likes the cookbook I'm working on."

"Cookbook?" questions Bobby. She really does have a voice. "We were actually mentioning this to Freddy the other day. What do you have in mind?"

Holy shit! I'm on a roll with this new career. I guess at sixty I've finally found my niche. "How does *Fanny on Fire* sound to you?" I inquire. "Believe it or not, in my spare time I've been indexing and refining a bunch of the recipes from the show. I'll use many of my own creations and some from the guests as well."

I've received standing ovations before in my other career (which you'll learn about in time), but when Myrna, Bobby, Freddy, Mandiyee, Puff, Duni-B, and the others all applauded, I felt like I was running naked with Solly in a large vat of dark chocolate hot fudge. What could be more delicious? And quite the cash cow for FUC…

eight

David Tobin and the Doomed Domestic Bliss

Today's episode deals with *pareve* (kosher foods that can be eaten with either meat or dairy) dishes. In demand is my *3Cs Crunchy Egg Salad*.

"For those of you who keep a kosher home, you can serve this dish as an appetizer before your main meat meal or with any dairy dish. Let's start chopping the celery. Oh shit…" Cut.

Next thing I know when I come to, is that Carlos, our beloved (and hefty) drag queen stagehand, brightly clad in his yellow satin hot pants, a pink and yellow striped crop top, with gold gladiator wedges, is *schlepping* me backstage while I'm spurting blood from my left hand. Once he gets me safely set in the doctor's office on the side of the studio—a must for all cooking shows and I just learned this the hard way—Carlos proceeds to faint and land with a thud on the gurney next to mine.

This is the first I've met Dr. Edelstein. She's a fairly young redhead and has a little trouble getting the bleeding to stop on my left hand long enough for her to inject a local anesthetic into my finger so she can stitch it shut. I make small talk with her because she looks nervous. "Not to worry; I've had two babies the natural way and no one is ever prepared for how gory that experience can be. Ouch, that stings." Hmmm…a redhead with *that* last name? Must be a *shikse* married to a Jew.

Soon my finger is numb and the nurse, who's blotting up the mess with gauze, gets my finger ready for the eight or so stitches Dr. Edelstein so deftly applies. Carlos is busy puking off the side of the other gurney and it's a circus as I hold his forehead with my right hand, while hoping my corpulent heroine, uh, hero, will soon feel better.

Though all of this took but forty-five minutes, I felt really badly about losing time on the set. So, since I was okay after a swig of brandy, I asked Freddy if we could just pick up where we left off with chopping the celery. Duni-B and Puff did the setup all over again. They cleaned up the bloody mess, cursed at me and each other under their breaths, and made sure everything looked exactly like it did when we began taping. But now I had this huge bandage covering my left middle finger. I would soon figure out a way to explain how it got there.

When I resumed chopping the celery, I mentioned the other ingredients, including hard boiled eggs, canola mayo, salt, pepper, ground mustard, celery, dried cranberries, and roasted cashews.

I did emphasize, "I like to use extra-large eggs. The bigger, the better," as I held up my two hands with palms to the ceiling. By accident, my thickly-bandaged middle finger stuck out and it looked like I was flipping the bird to the viewers. All I needed was the old Bronx cheer.

Of course, I seized that opportunity to blurt out, "Freakin' knives they give me here. They're sharp enough to start a *bris* (Jewish circumcision ceremony) business right here on the set. I guess I'm used to the smaller six-inch chef's knife I use at home in my kitchen. I've always told Solly that six inches is more than enough and they give me a ten-incher here? Way too big." Myrna and Bobby are rolling on the floor.

In late fall of 1977, David rented the smallest U-Haul trailer for $19.99 and hooked it up to his Eldorado. We brought what few possessions and clothing

I had from home, made one stop at Honig's Parkway in the Bronx to buy us a bed, and took a one-room studio apartment in a private house in Rye Brook, complete with hotplate and no kitchen. But after a week, the landlady—a fortyish spinster—who must have gotten fed up with the amorous noises coming from the back room with a separate entrance, found out that I was living there as well and gave David an eviction notice. Not sure if she was jealous or had sights on David before she realized he was in a relationship.

David and I had just one week to find another place. We took a second floor, one-bedroom apartment in an old residential neighborhood in Port Chester, New York. The landlady, an Italian-American widow in her sixties, lived on the first floor. The walls were quite thin and Mrs. Lauria used to cry for her mama in her sleep almost every night.

By then, I was working for Kobor International Corporation in Larchmont, New York, as an import clerk. We used to get up at around seven a.m. and, in good weather, walk up the steep hill to VJ's to enjoy our breakfast together. It was usually something that would kill me now, almost forty years later, with greasy bacon, heavily buttered toast, and fried eggs. But VJ, the old chef, had a knack for oily cuisine. David would then leave for IBM in Yorktown Heights and I drove to Kobor in Larchmont not too far away.

One year, for my birthday, David bought me a four-piece set of Teflon non-stick cooking pans, quite the rage at the time, because he was just so thoughtful and knew I had expressed an interest in learning to cook like VJ. Back then no one knew, and few cared, that those pans were carcinogenic. I was touched and thrilled. David always used to do sweet things like that. More likely, though, David might have been wishing that with new pans I'd learn to cook something other than my *Yum-mush* which by then was getting old.

Of the many things that Kobor imported, cashew nuts were the chief commodity. Within the office, the lab assistant used to test the raw cashews by roasting them and then salting them. If they passed the tests, the cashews would be sold to leading nut companies throughout the United States. Often, I would get paper bags of hot roasted cashews to take home so we could enjoy them for dessert in the evenings. One day I left a fresh bag on the windowsill overnight and awoke to find bugs crawling out of it, down the wall, all over the kitchen table, and into our fruit bowl. I screamed for David while gagging and coming quite close to throwing up all over the creepy crawlers. Apparently, the chemist slipped up on that batch. It took me about twenty years before I'd eat another cashew, but now it's one of my favorite ingredients to use in specialty dishes.

I remember Kobor International's after-work, in-office holiday party. Everyone was drinking and eating from the abundant, fancy cold-cut platters catered by the German deli down the street. We were all loose, relaxed, and telling jokes. No import-export documents needed tending to at *this* party. In my early twenties and feeling quite sexy, I decided to see if I could make the normally nine-to-five, sour-faced, early sixtyish Mr. Gottlieb smile. He was always serious and always on the phone and Helen, the office gossip, told me he was once a Jew who converted to something I had never heard of—Ethical Culture.

"What the hell is that?" I asked her. "Either you're a Jew or you're a *goy* (not Jewish, Gentile)!" Anyway, after dessert was served and everyone—further fueled—was even happier, I went over to Mr. Gottlieb's desk and asked him if Helen could snap a picture of us for the Kobor newsletter. I ran to sit on his lap while Helen said, "Say cheese." Mr. Gottlieb had the biggest shit-eating grin, the likes of which I've never seen since that office party so many years ago. I still have that picture to this day.

After several months in our little apartment, there was a violent rainstorm and because we lived on the top floor, the roof began first to drip, then leak by bucketsful through the ceiling of our little bedroom. At three a.m. David had to run downstairs and knock on Mrs. Lauria's door to see if she could get her son-in-law, who worked in construction and lived in a house in the back of the property, to fix the leak. She just looked at us in half-asleep shock and handed us a bucket. "What do you expect me to do, have Johnny go up on the roof now in the storm in the middle of the night?" Point taken. No sleep that night between emptying the buckets into the bathtub about every fifteen minutes and listening to Mrs. Lauria scream for her mama.

After about a year and a half of domestic bliss, David began to come home drunk. Occasionally, he would go to a pub in Elmsford after work with co-workers but would normally have only one Dewar's and water to relax. He participated in the first generation of computer robotics at IBM in the seventies and at times the job could be stressful. Lately, he would have more than one, and one evening I watched him wobble upstairs to our second-floor entrance with a black eye. Naturally, I was worried because I loved him. David, ever sweet and even-tempered, was never violent. He said he got into a tiff with one of his pub mates. It never dawned on me that something else might be bothering him beyond the stress of research in a new computer field.

Remember David's concern about our age difference which originally led me into the arms of Freddy then back into David's again? Well, now I was almost twenty-five and my selfless David began to think once again…Fanny should get married and have children. So, we had *the talk*. Certainly not a talk I'd wanted to have back then. Like a déjà vu, but about two and a half years after the original.

Said David, "I know you don't want to have kids now, but someday you will. I already have my son, Scott, and I don't want any more children. As much as I love you, I want you to learn to be more independent, to live on your own, and meet someone closer to your own age." Was I ever sad? I felt like a steamroller had just run over my heart.

I tried to get David to reconsider. I was afraid to live on my own and there was no way I was going to return to dysfunctional life in the Bronx. By then, David had helped me begin weekly therapy sessions with Ida Asher in White Plains. Next week's would be a doozy.

Soon, David found a small, yellow-painted, old studio apartment in Lincolndale, New York, near his work. He drove me up there one evening after a lovely farewell dinner and we slow-danced to "Honesty" sung by Billy Joel on the radio. We both cried and then loved passionately. David promised to always be there for me, that we'd stay in touch, and that he'd be my friend *for life*. How prophetic that would prove to be, almost thirty years later.

nine

Boris Perlmutter and the "Oops!"

Solly and I were playing around in our huge kitchen at home in New Jersey as I tested recipes for my new book. I wanted to include something delicious and hearty for breakfast because I knew I would have one or two breakfast chapters. I like fairly easy recipes. If they're not simple, I usually don't make them. For me, Jewish cooking is simple and tasty. The more the ingredients, the likelier they are to be dumped into my slow cooker, and then I'm done.

Then, for some strange reason, I remembered this one guy who was obsessed with oatmeal for breakfast. Some people like variety...omelets, eggs and toast, maybe even *blintzes* (thin, pancake-like crepe filled with either fruit or cheese, then fried) if you feel like using the packaged, frozen variety, because who the fuck wants to futz around when you first get up out of bed? I have enough with my damned insomnia.

Yes, Boris Perlmutter used to eat oatmeal for breakfast every day, but with *salt*. Salty oatmeal? As far as I'm concerned, there's only one warm, white, gooey liquid that should be salty, and it's not oatmeal.

Well, Solly loves caramel, and salted caramel sauce seems to be the rage. "*Tahteleh* (Little Daddy, a loving term, sometimes used for a father or son)," I asked. "How does oatmeal with pecans and salted caramel sauce sound to you?"

Solly came over to me, grabbed me in his arms, and said, "Sure, my *Fanneleh.* Anything you make will be delicious. And when you're done, we can use the sauce as edible body paint." At this age, I love a man with a good imagination…

After David moved to Lincolndale, he called me at least once a week and often came for a visit if he was doing something in Westchester County. I stayed living in Mrs. Lauria's second-floor apartment, but couldn't stand the landlady screaming in her sleep and keeping me awake at night. At that time, my brother, Marty, who did shift work in the late seventies, had turned me on to a great invention that I use to this day—a white noise machine. It helped drown out external noises. Now there's even a phone app for that. I gave notice that I was moving and since leases in private homes were not popular back then, it was fairly easy. I moved out in early 1979 with the help of David and a few other friends.

My new apartment was affordable…$200 per month plus utilities. It was on Touraine Avenue, also in an old residential neighborhood on the other side of Port Chester, a few blocks away from Route 1. Of course, I had no experience with renting or what to look for in an apartment, but I soon found out why the rent was so cheap. It was a one-bedroom apartment—a third floor walk-up in an old stone six-family house. And there was no heat to speak of. The center room of the apartment was a huge kitchen. To one side of the kitchen, there was a door that led to the living room and to the other side of the kitchen was a door that led to the bedroom and bathroom. In the kitchen, there was a stove with a heater that was *supposed* to heat the entire apartment. It never did, especially when it was below fifty degrees outside.

During winters, I'd have to use a portable space heater every night in the bedroom; and because it was electric, it doubled my utilities so that they exceeded my rent costs in the wintertime. I used to carry that little heater around with me into the bathroom whenever I took my sit-down "showers" and got ready for work in the mornings. The old clawed bath tub had no shower, so I had to rig a rubber hose to the faucet just to wash my hair. Needless to say, the floor got wet constantly because I couldn't think of a way to install a shower curtain that didn't look stupid for just a bath tub. I probably could have gotten electrocuted from the splashes of water near the space heater, but warmth overruled common sense back then.

I made up my mind it was time to leave my job at Kobor International when the wealthy owner, Ted Kobor, decided he had permission to cop a feel of my ass the time I entered his office to deliver some import-export documents for signature. Granted, I was in my mid-twenties and did go braless because I hated bras—but teasing men—at least married ones—was not my mission. I was no one's property just because he owned the company and he *thought* he had the right to touch me.

As I look back, I should have gone straight to his wife who was friendly and frequently visited the office. But I was just shocked and caught off guard. And, as you know by now, back then I typically acted instinctually. So, I quit. Besides, Mrs. Kobor probably knew about her husband's indiscretions and chose to ignore them for the lifestyle of the rich and famous. Of course, I told my female co-workers why, as if to give them a warning to be on the lookout for the boss. It just felt good to get it off of my braless chest.

Fortunately, the import-export job market was decent in the late seventies and I went on an interview almost immediately to yet another Jewish-owned small business in Harrison, New York. I wore a simple, knee-length coral skirt, a coral and turquoise knitted vest over a white button-down blouse, and of course, *no bra*. I was only a B-cup so I didn't flop around too much, but apparently it was enough to get hired. On the spot. By then, I did, however, have several years of international trade experience on my résumé.

Chemical Commodities was a business owned by Ivan Strasser, a Jewish immigrant from Germany. The vice president who hired me was Mendel Strassman, also a German Jewish immigrant, and I was amused by the similarity in their names. Everyone was pleasant, especially the owner, Ivan, who promoted me to office manager shortly after I was hired. He was tall, skinny, gray-haired, and about sixty. He then proceeded to have a heart attack and died after I had been working there for only about three months. The office girls joked and said that my *tansing* (dancing) around the office braless every day must have killed him. So sad—he was a nice guy.

Meanwhile, the vice president, Mendel, a sweet fiftyish family man, worked very closely with me to teach me how to import chemicals from all over the world. I enjoyed it and learned an awful lot about regulations involved in logistics—the moving of various commodities around the world. Prior to this, as you know, I had imported fish, bicycles, and cashews. I learned that there were different regulations for different commodities and also learned that I enjoyed working with people from different countries. Having studied Spanish, French, and Italian in high school and at New York University, I had a knack for languages and was even able to help translate Portuguese shipping documents that came in—by mail, of course, no email, not even faxes yet. Import-export was a great field for a person with OCD tendencies because of minute details that could mean the difference between a shipment clearing customs, being held up, or even returned to the country of origin.

Summers, we used to take three-hour-long lunches, and Mendel would take a few of us co-workers with him on his boat in the nearby harbor. Missy, the Jewish bookkeeper, used to entertain us with funny stories in Yiddish of her escapades all over Long Island from where she commuted just two days a week since she was semi-retired. One time, she told us a story about how Jews would fill the local Chinese restaurants on Christmas to eat pork, spare ribs, and other delicacies that were taboo in their kosher homes. Everyone was laughing so hard that the boat rocked, and Missy fell off the side. Mendel had to jump into the fairly shallow water to help her back into the boat.

Content at my job and supporting myself in my walk-up apartment, it was time to meet a nice guy like David wanted for me. In addition to visiting Intro by Camera in White Plains, one evening Sara Ornstein, my friend who used to work with me at Togi America, phoned me to say there was a Jewish singles dance being held at Club 69 on the East Side near Sutton Place on Saturday night. I really didn't like singles dances because more often than not, guys would end up on one side of the room and the girls on the other side with only a few couples dancing in the center on the dance floor. Just like those high school dances so many years back. However, I said, "What the hell," and drove down to Pelham Parkway to pick Sara up for our drive to the city. Back then, it was a lot easier to find metered parking and we found a spot not too far away from the club.

Sara and I checked our coats, paid the five-dollar entrance fee, and sat down on two vacant bar stools in the center of the bar. Almost immediately, a cute but fairly short brown-haired guy approached me, extended his hand to shake, and introduced himself as Boris Perlmutter. He said he was an accountant at Brooklyn College and lived in Brooklyn. Good, I thought. Probably earns a decent living. At this point in my mid-twenties, per David's "orders," I began to weed out the undesirables in an effort to find marriage material.

As I told him about myself, I said I was from the Bronx and lived and worked in Westchester. The reason I included the Westchester tidbit is that I didn't want the distance to be an obstacle. We spoke about our mutual interest in classic country music, danced to a few songs, and he took my number. It was late in the holiday season, so he immediately asked me out for New Year's Eve. I figured, what the heck. One of the reasons Sara and I went to the dance so close to the end of the year was to find someone with whom to go *out with the old, and in with the new*. Hmmm, I thought, out and in, out and in, out and in…

As it got later, around midnight, I looked over at Sara who was dancing with a freckled red-headed guy whom she nicknamed "Gingy," and gave her the signal it was time to drive home. She was grateful because she didn't like the guy. Sara later told me she didn't care for redheads but liked the Rod Stewart song "Do Ya Think I'm Sexy," so she agreed to *just* dance. We said goodnight to a few friends we knew from the crowd and Boris Perlmutter gave me a kiss on the cheek. "See you on New Year's Eve." Okay…a new adventure for Fanny.

Cut to New Year's Eve, December 31, 1979. Boris had a white 1977 Mercury Cougar and it was a snazzy car. He immediately got one point for that. He had driven the hour or so from Brooklyn to Port Chester and when he knocked on my door he was a little out of breath from climbing the three flights of old and rickety stairs. I peeped through the chain lock, saw it was Boris, and let him in. He smiled and said I looked pretty. I was wearing a gray velvet top with black satin slacks and my typical sterling silver assortment of blingy jewelry. My black heels made me slightly taller than Boris. Later on, when my shoes would come off, all things would equalize, I was sure.

Off we went to a Chinese restaurant, Ting Ling, in Mamaroneck. I had eaten there several times before with David and it had the best Chinese food in the area. Boris took my coat and held my chair for me while I sat down. Hmm, another point for manners.

We looked at the menu and, naturally, I mentioned the pork dishes. Boris confessed to keeping "semi-kosher." What the F did that mean? He said that when he ate out, he would eat meats that weren't kosher or fish, but at home, he would only eat kosher meats and absolutely *no pork* under any circumstances. Oh well, so that might limit what I could cook if I ever decided to make him something at my apartment. But so far, we were off to an okay start. I, of course, had pork egg foo young—my palate was not very sophisticated back then—and he had a vegetarian stir-fry of some sort with rice. But I couldn't share my plate with him.

After dinner we came back to my place and watched a little TV, starting out in the cold living room with Boris's arm around me. The kitchen's heater stove was on but pumping inadequate, cold air. By around 11:45 p.m. we approached my bedroom with my trusty little electric space heater, turned on the Dick Clark New Year's Eve special on channel seven, and started making out. Decent kisser. Midnight, January 1, 1980: Happy New Year wishes being exchanged by loud Times Square revelers on TV and from Boris Perlmutter.

Boris was seven years older, never married, and quirky. When he went to pee, he used toilet paper to wipe himself instead of just shaking dry like most males. I also noticed he put salt on his oatmeal, which was the only thing he'd have every morning for breakfast when he stayed over.

Eventually, Boris and I saw each other every weekend—it was easier for him to drive up to Port Chester than for him to pick me up, then *schlep* me back to Brooklyn. By the end of January, I had missed my period. Before this, I was like clockwork. I had used a Copper 7 IUD ever since I was with Simon in the mid-seventies. With Boris, just to be sure, we used a condom as well.

By February 1, I still hadn't gotten my visitor, so I told Boris. I made an appointment to see Nadine Conservus, my gynecologist from Suriname, who practiced in New Rochelle. Boris came with me and the doctor took urine but wanted to take some blood to be certain. Here I was, twenty-five and scared shitless of needles. Since I had no choice, I held out my arm and said, "Fire away."

I was surprised that it didn't hurt, but was floored when, after examining me, she said, "You're pregnant, and probably due sometime in October." Right now, I didn't have time for any emotions. Without a minute's hesitation, Boris and I both asked her about abortions, which we knew she performed at the Jewish Memorial Hospital in Upper Manhattan. *Roe v. Wade* had recently taken them out of the back rooms where coat hangers were once used.

What were the odds? I had an IUD and we used a condom as well. Oh shit...

ten

The Scandalous Pork Break-Up

At that recent, surprisingly wonderful FUC meeting, Myrna suggested I come up with one or two more unique recipes. I'm considering working on a chicken dish since the only recipe I have for poultry, so far, is *Grammy Jane's Jewish Penicillin*, which she wrote by hand for me a few years before she died. That might be hard, though, because I don't eat chicken (or turkey, or duck, or any fowl, for that matter), so I can't taste while I cook. Every good chef knows that's a must. Dark meat chicken is easy; maybe I'll do that. Maybe I'll get Solly to come in and taste me, uh, taste *for* me.

Wait. Know what just came to me? The time I made a breakup dinner for Boris Perlmutter, who never ate *treyf*. Well, at least not willingly. Or should I say, he never ate pork, but ate *treyf* outside of his home whenever *he* decided it was okay. For some reason, chicken or beef didn't have to be kosher. He made his own rules and I never understood them.

Yes, that's it. *Scandalous Pork Tenderloin*, with six cloves of garlic, honey and soy sauce. Tastes just like dark meat chicken, so I'm told. Only pork can never be kosher. All the Jews I know, like me, partake of the pig. Of course there are Jews who don't, but remember, this isn't a *kosher* cooking show. I'm thinking Myrna will consider this unique, at least for a Jewish-*style* cooking show.

We went back to my place and talked. We were not married and it was way too early in our relationship for us to even consider it. So we agreed to arrange an appointment for Dr. Conservus to do the deed. I was scared and told no one other than Cami, and of course, David, whom I still saw and spoke with regularly.

On Thursday night, February 14, Boris came to my apartment and brought me a huge box of chocolates and a card for Valentine's Day in an effort to cheer me up. My emotions were all over the place. I don't think I was sad. I was more scared of the unknown than of anything else. Would it hurt? Would I bleed? Would anyone find out?

Friday morning, February 15, 1980, Boris drove us to Jewish Memorial Hospital and I followed strict orders not to have anything to eat or drink after midnight the evening before. Boris took off from work and I called in sick, seriously hoping that I'd be okay over the weekend enough to go back to work by Monday. We met with Dr. Conservus and I put on one of those stupid faded, pastel-colored, open-backed gowns where your ass sticks out. Why the hell do they have tie-strings on them if you can't really shut the back?

One of the nurses prepped me and started an IV—again with the damn needles—and next thing I knew, I was awake and resting in a bed in a recovery room with Boris by my side eating a grilled cheese sandwich. I was fortunate to feel okay enough to say, "I'm starved; let's go to Levi's Deli in Riverdale so I can have some brisket." Here I just aborted a child and I was still thinking about food.

When the doctor said it was okay to leave, she gave me a box of sanitary napkins as I had no idea I'd be bleeding afterward. I was just glad there was no pain—physical, that is. I'd have plenty of emotional pain for many years to come.

Since all was over by about ten a.m., Boris drove me back to Port Chester, made sure I was okay, and then raced back to Brooklyn College because he had an important project to complete with a deadline. I was okay with that. Besides, David came right over after work and stayed with me all night to make sure I was okay. Boris knew that David was just an old friend.

Eventually, it hit me. While I was pregnant for such a brief time, I did feel that I was too young to take responsibility for anyone other than myself. Legal abortion made life dispensable. But afterward, I felt such a deep, indescribable loss for which I did not give myself any time to mourn. My hormones went haywire. I would frequently sob into David's arms and he would always comfort me by joking, "Look, I told you to find someone to marry *first*, and *then* have a baby. You got the order all wrong."

I went back to work the following Monday and I was okay but sad. Boris suggested we do a little traveling—a change of scenery might do us both good.

During the spring, we went on a long weekend to Atlantic City, stayed at the Resorts International which was in its heyday, and walked along the boardwalk. I still have pictures from those pseudo-happy times.

In the summer of 1980, Boris and I planned a ten-day trip throughout the state of Texas. I had accumulated some vacation time from Chemical Commodities, so in July we flew into Houston. I was in love with the movie *Urban Cowboy* and wanted our first stop to be Gilley's, the honky-tonk in Pasadena—just outside of Houston—made popular by that movie starring John Travolta and Debra Winger.

Boris and I had practiced the Texas Two-Step over and over in my living room to the soundtrack for a few weeks prior to the trip. I even bought a cheap denim cowboy hat which was the first indication that I wasn't a local because everyone at Gilley's wore Stetsons. The second giveaway was when Boris and I did a slow dance, clockwise, smack in the middle of the sawdust-covered dance floor, and the hordes began to push us aside as they did a rapid, counter-clockwise two-step along the outside rim. "Dang those Yankees," we heard, but fortunately there were no bar room brawls like in the movie. We quietly retreated to the gift shop to buy souvenirs.

To this day, my daughter, Lori, has my beautiful ecru-colored leather cowboy boots with the turquoise-inlaid butterflies that I wore thirty-five years ago at Gilley's. She's a full shoe size smaller than I but loves the boots so much she wears two pairs of socks whenever she puts them on.

Over the next few days, we visited with my local Houston cousins and went to the flea market at the old AstroWorld amusement park where I had a meltdown. We sat down on a black wrought-iron bench in a beautiful, flower-lined section of the park and I just sobbed. It was obvious to Boris what was happening and he just hugged me and clearly said, "You know we couldn't have a child now, but one day we'll get married and have a baby." Was I *ever* naïve? I believed him at the time. I calmed down a bit and we proceeded with our vacation.

We drove our way west to San Antonio in the rain, listening to Eddie Rabbit's "Driving My Life Away" on the AM radio station in our rental car. The sights and sounds of the River Walk were colorful, and we later toured the Alamo. We walked the outdoor *mercados* (street markets). During breakfast at our hotel, Perlmutter—I had taken to calling him that when he wasn't around—would always have his salted oatmeal. I guess he thought it was his only choice since he didn't eat bacon or sausage with eggs.

We went to quite a few really good Mexican restaurants in and around San Antonio and he was careful not to eat anything *treyf*, but in his eyes, that just meant *no pork*. Apparently, chicken was okay even if it was difficult to find a kosher Mexican restaurant in San Antonio in those days. I didn't understand his reasoning, but I never said anything. I was still numb from all that had happened, I guess.

We then drove up north to Dallas-Fort Worth via Austin. I always watched *Austin City Limits* on TV for the great music and wanted to stop there and on to Waco because I wanted to see the Brazos River made popular by a famous country music song. Our trip ended, after a total of ten days, at the DFW airport, where we flew back to New York.

The scenery of the trip was gorgeous and memorable. But I could not feel happy. I was looking forward to getting back to work, and after a few weeks back in New York, when Boris and I were just waking up one Saturday morning, my phone rang.

"Fanny, this is Simon. I'm in New York and I want to see you before I go back to Israel." Boris was half asleep and turned over to listen.

"I hear you got married two years ago and you have a little boy. Why are you calling me here?" I asked, really pissed off. I found out later on that he called Mommy in the Bronx and for some stupid reason she gave him my number in Port Chester. He was in the United States by himself on a vacation from Israel.

"Well, I just thought we could be friends," he said. I told him not to call me anymore. Was I ever glad I broke off that engagement three years earlier. Had I married Simon, he would have been doing the same thing to me that he was doing to his Israeli wife, that he did to Arlene Gladstein, and probably even to me when he was on leave in Tijuana before he was discharged from the Navy. He was a serial cheater—a polygamist. I was so lucky I never caught any sexually transmitted diseases from him. Boris overheard everything and although I did nothing wrong, he began to mistrust me.

That morning, he suggested we take a month-long break from each other. Having been devoid of emotion for the past several months for obvious reasons, I wasn't even shocked. He walked to the door, said, "I'll be in touch," and didn't even eat his salty fucking oatmeal that was congealing on the stove.

I've never been one to like a man calling the shots, especially in such a negative way, so what was the first thing I did? I made an appointment to go back to Intro by Camera and make full use of my lifetime membership.

During Perlmutter's month-long hiatus, I met two really nice guys. Both were named Aaron and both lived in Rockland County, New York, over the Tappan Zee Bridge. One was Aaron R., who had long brown hair, a mustache, and a beard—yes, my type. The other was Aaron S., who had black hair and was tall, skinny, and clean-shaven. Aaron R. took me to see *Evita* on Broadway with Patty Lupone and Mandy Patinkin (another Jewish hunk). Aaron S. used to bring me flowers for every date and took me to a most memorable Mickey Gilley concert.

This dating thing was lots of fun, but it was getting tiresome. I really did want to settle down. Eventually, the Aaron R. thing fizzled out and Aaron S. asked me to come to his condo in Rockland for a visit. He wanted me to move in with him. He had a dog. I've always been allergic to dogs, though it's much worse now that I'm older. I figured I'd give it a shot. We went to dinner on a Saturday night, then back to his place. I immediately began to itch from hives and started wheezing. Shit, just as I'd thought.

This poor guy must have been really smitten because he even said, "Fanny, I'll get rid of this dog for *you.*" What was I, the Queen of England? I thanked him, but as he drove me home I explained that we probably shouldn't see each other. He said he'd call me, and he did, but I didn't feel like having an asthma attack every time he kissed me because the dog had licked his face before he came over.

Meanwhile, in the early fall of 1980, since I was following David's orders and thought I'd found someone, I decided to do a good deed and try to find David a girlfriend. There was this newfangled computer dating thing that had just become popular, so I gave him a brochure about it I'd found in a display in the lobby of the Neptune Diner in White Plains. You'd complete an application with your interests, goals, and hobbies and mail it in. Within a week or so, you'd get a list of potential dates with similar goals and interests. The match was *supposedly* made by a computer.

Almost immediately, David not only met Elsie, a hot, blonde flight attendant, but they got married within less than a month. She also forced him to have a vasectomy because she had already had three husbands by the age of thirty-seven and six abortions before they'd met. And she knew that children would interfere with her lifestyle. I'll tell you more about that tragedy later on. But what bothered me most was, while Boris never gave a shit that I was still friends with David, a very insecure Elsie forbade David from being my forever friend. Had that little glitch not occurred, my life might not have followed the course it did, leading to marriage number one, a few years later.

The last time I saw David, in 1980, was when he came to my apartment to recuperate from his vasectomy, and every hour I had to change the ice packs the doctor had ordered to reduce swelling in his testicles. Now, with the only true confidant out of my life, I was on my own. Anger gave way to emotional strength-building and baby steps towards many years of cynicism. Wow, I thought, Elsie had David, literally, by the balls.

The Perlmutter month-long hiatus was up and I had a colorful bouquet from Aaron S. sitting in a vase, quite freshly- and well-preserved, in the center of my living room with the door to the kitchen closed. It was as cold as a florist's refrigerator in that room since the heat from the kitchen stove apparatus couldn't get in with the door closed. When Boris Perlmutter called on his way, my emotions began to swell—and not in a good way—so I began to plan a revenge dinner...

Boris walked in, kissed and hugged me, and we made some small talk. I played along with the jovial atmosphere when, in reality, I was seething that it was *he* who called the shots on our month-long hiatus. First, the baby-daddy phobia, the promise of a future together, then a time out...who the fuck did he think he was? If we were meant to be, a month-long break wouldn't mean a damn thing.

I told him I made sliced dark meat chicken with honey, soy sauce, and garlic. "Yum. This is great," he said with a mouthful. After dinner at the big kitchen table, he got up to stretch and he walked over to open the living room door. I'd always kept it closed to save money on heating bills, which as I mentioned were quite costly with that little electric space heater. I only used the living room for parties.

"*Who* gave you flowers?" Did he expect I'd be a month-long monk?

Not wanting to deal with the bullshit, I just said, "My boss Mendel wanted to celebrate a new customer we got at work, so he gave me flowers."

I calmly walked over to the front door, opened the chain, and said goodbye to Boris forever. And on his way out, as he was about to descend the staircase in the hallway, I shouted, "I hope you enjoyed the *pork. Gey kocken aufen yam* (Go shit in the ocean), you *momzer* (bastard)!"

73

The look on his face was priceless as his eyes bugged out and his mouth formed a shocked "Oh!"

eleven

It's Raining Men

The Blind Mother Truckers, one of the most famous country music groups *ever*, has recently been inducted into the Willie Nelson-Dolly Parton Country Music Honor Society. They've been touring the nation for several months on their *Beat the Meat* tour. The name was taken from their mega hit single, "Mama Beat Daddy, and Daddy Beat the Meat."

As you'll soon learn, I've always been a huge country music fan. Recently, I heard Bobby singing along to "Beat the Meat" as she played air guitar. It was quite the sight. I said to her, "Damn, you can really move those hips!"

And without missing a beat, Bobby said, straight-faced, "That's exactly what my wife says." She added, "Our friend, Bruce, knows their agent. Maybe we can get them on the show when they come to New York."

I immediately replied, "I'd just *plotz* (collapse with emotion)," and Bobby grinned.

Wouldn't you know, five weeks later Bobby worked her magic and Wilbur Stone, Calvin Smith, and Shorty Brooks were about to walk on the set. I made sure I had taken half a Xanax before the show because the idea of meeting such famous country stars made me nervous. Sometimes, Xanax loosened my lips a bit, but I figured I'd take a chance.

75

The set was ready thanks to Duni-B and Puff who kept taking cross-eyed selfies to post on Instagram, complaining about a boring hick music group.

"Friends, today's cooking guests are the super famous Blind Motherfuc, uh, Mother Truckers. Meet Wilbur Stone, Calvin Smith, and Shorty Brooks." Wilbur and Calvin walk out, each with the aid of twin seeing-eye dogs, and Shorty, a little person less than four feet tall, uses a tiny cane with a red tip. Prior to today, I had only heard their voices, so I had no idea they were all sightless.

"Welcome boys, *achooo*. Shit, I'm allergic to dogs. I should've taken a Benadryl instead of a Xanax. I'm a huge fan. Wilbur and Calvin, you each stand next to me. Shorty, why don't you get up on this stool so at least we can see your face, even if you can't see mine." Oops.

"Today's masterpiece is *Beef Noodle Soup with Snow Peas and Orzo*."

We proceed to talk about how much they like meat, steak, and beef in general. They were meat and potatoes kind of men. I ask Calvin to take a pinch of salt and pepper and rub it on the stir-fry beef. "This will tenderize it a bit, as that cut tends to be a bit tough." He takes his two hands and starts feeling around the table, but first takes his left hand and grabs my boob. I slap it off and tell him, "Now Calvin, grab the meat, not my boob."

Once he locates the salt and pepper, he does a fine job. "Wow, Calvin. You're really good at rubbing that meat," I say. Shorty, next to me, immediately pipes in with a squeaky voice sounding like a southern leprechaun, and says, "Where do you think we got the title of our hit song?"

When the set is over and everyone has tasted and enjoyed the soup, thankfully our lecherous musical guests move, with the help of their dogs and Shorty's mini-cane, to the adjacent stage to start their song. The backdrop has the group's logo—a 3-D photo of an eighteen-wheeler with huge dark glasses wrapped around the front of the rig.

Shorty creates the beat by fingering the washboard, "One-two-three-four," while Calvin and Wilbur strum their guitars and Bobby, behind the cameras, starts shaking her ass. "After all them years, ahm jest bone-tired, cuz livin' with y'all ain't been no easy feat. That's why ahm a-leavin', ahm a-leavin' home. Cuz mama beat daddy and daddy beat the meat."

During 1980 and 1981, Fanny Goldman took on Intro by Camera with a vengeance. I was working at Chemical Commodities, enjoying life but missing David, and dating up a storm. Sure, I had my share of colorful suitors—dates every weekend, now even more abundant with my lifetime membership to Mack Sabatino's dating service. While many mid-twenties gals might be satisfied with that lifestyle, I felt unfulfilled. Something was missing.

Let's see. First, there was Carson Fitzgerald. A nice enough Irish-American guy who lived in Cortlandt Manor, New York, and loved Jewish girls. We dated for a few months. He was intelligent enough and had a nice smile. But once we got to the bedroom, his kinkiness was a bit much. You see, he liked to be spanked and he liked to spank. "Who's been naughty?" Not Fanny. I managed to fix him up with an acquaintance of mine who lived in the Bronx and was on the verge of becoming a spinster. Believe it or not, the two hit it off. Go figure.

Then, there was Darren Rosenberg, a dark-haired lumpy sort who spoke with a nasal whine. He had a whole videotaping studio set up in his bedroom in a condo in Rye, New York. "No, I will not be taped in the act, thank you very much," I said. I guess now I can see why he had such elaborate equipment in his bedroom; must have been to compensate for his having to use specialty Forex lambskin condoms, size *extra-small*. Where's the magnifying glass?

After Darren, I dated a twin named Jonah Salzberg, originally from Long Island, who had an apartment in nearby Greenburgh, New York. He had a thing for dressing up like Alice Cooper, complete with black eye shadow and black wig. One weekend he and I went to his parents' summer house on the lake in Danbury, Connecticut. He clearly indicated that they wouldn't be there that weekend.

Much to my surprise, however, when we arrived we found his twin brother, Carl, hanging out. I had no idea how he got there because he didn't drive as Jonah said he was slightly mentally challenged. But boy was he a hunk just like his brother. Both were over six feet tall, dark brown hair, lean and lanky, and mirror images. Who cared about his limited intelligence? We shared a few joints and soon I was ready for my first ménage à trois. But Carl, who had never had a girlfriend, just went off to watch TV and my date, Jonah, split to don his Alice Cooper costume. Next in line...

Randy Diamond was the most gorgeous potential twin brother to Harry Reems, my all-time favorite famed Jewish porn star. We had planned to meet for our first date the summer of 1981 at the entrance gates to Rye Playland amusement park. Since we both had seen each other's videotapes, my heart began to flutter as I saw Randy approach, walking from the parking lot to the ticket booths where I was standing. From his short-sleeved green polo shirt, open at the top three buttons, I could see he had a hairy, muscular body, and the delicious brown Harry Reems mustache brought about nirvana. His form-fitting jeans revealed a perfect ass, as well as a nicely-shaped ample wad up front.

I had on a tight red tube top, no bra (duh), matching red lipstick, size seven blue, butt-hugging denim short-shorts, and my chocolate brown, high-heeled Candies clogs, which were the rage at the time. My daughter, Lori, inherited those years ago since I no longer wear heels. Remember, I told you I was blessed with fucked-up feet, probably as a result of wearing all of those stilettos in my youth. It most likely was genetic, though, because Mommy never wore heels either on her size eleven feet. But damn, those Candies shoes were made well—Lori still has them—unlike shoes that are made in China these days. I'll tell you more about my knowledge of products made in China later on.

The sizzle with Randy was immediate. We went on a few rides at Playland while I thought of him riding *me*, and then we started kissing like horny teens in the Tunnel of Love. When it began to get dark outside, he asked to come back to my place, and since I lived *really* close by—less than ten minutes away—I thought, why not? It wouldn't have been practical at the time to drive all the way up to Ridgefield, Connecticut, where Randy had a beautiful house. We were in the mood *now*.

It was easy to see this would be an intense physical relationship. I had my own personal porn star. A few weeks later we went out to dinner, then back to his house. Poor guy; his house was bare and tired-looking. He didn't even have a bar of soap in the house when we went to take a bath. He drove out looking for a 7-11, but everything was closed as he lived in a fairly rural area. I knew from Intro by Camera that he was a widower, but he eventually told me the story. He lost his pregnant wife, a nurse at Yonkers Hospital, in a car crash as she was walking across a busy street. That accounted, though, for the vacant house. His life was empty. So sad.

We saw each other a few times after that, and with each date there was the same powerful, raw magnetism. We were filling each other's emptiness. One day, Randy called to tell me about the anti-Semitism he had been facing for a long while at his job in Weston, Connecticut. Local rednecks would leave swastikas and "Jew bastard" signs painted on his locker at the post office where he was a mail sorter. Between the death of his wife and the daily prejudice he encountered at work, he was about to burst and just wanted to get away.

He was planning on leaving within a week or two, taking his motorcycle, and driving practically cross-country in a life-changing move to Tucson, Arizona. Would I come with him? Well, I seriously thought about it, but although I'd miss the animal attraction I felt for this guy, I didn't want to leave my job and my family and friends in New York. "Sorry, Randy, no can do. I wish you happiness and a good life."

After Randy, there was Henry Tendler who was a cute, wealthy patent attorney with law offices in Mount Vernon, New York. He had never married and was ten years older. This was already a red flag since most guys back then had been married and divorced by his age, thirty-seven. He had wispy, thinning light brown hair and of course, a mustache. A waterfront condo in the Throggs Neck area of the Bronx wasn't shabby either. For our first date, he drove up in a shiny, new model, beige Cadillac and took me to The Sign of the Dove, a snazzy east-side restaurant, where we ate *Duck à l'Orange*—yes, I still ate poultry back then. Talk about impressing a gal. Henry was well-spoken but seemed just a bit effeminate.

No matter, I thought, this was the life. Henry would pick me up and we'd go to the most elite places this Bronx Jewish girl had never before experienced. He invited me to take a trip with him to his winter home, a beachside condo in Lake Worth, Florida. This trip was the beginning of my lifelong affinity for and genetic predisposition to southeast Florida. He drove me around The Breakers in Palm Beach as my jaw dropped from such opulence. We sunned on his terrace while I wore my skimpy purple bikini.

But when it came to the bedroom, he did not *come*. Literally. He liked to kiss, but that was all. Could I be content with just kissing? Not at twenty-seven. Nope. I took a deep breath and mustered up the courage to ask him, trying to be polite and unintimidating, if he had ever had a sexual relationship with a lady.

I had to hand it to him. The poor guy confessed that, while he liked to kiss, he was asexual. He said, "Everyone likes to kiss." I was dumbfounded as I had never before heard that term, and certainly never personally encountered anyone who was asexual. I couldn't even compare him to Hernando Santiago, my first boyfriend, because although he, too, was effeminate, I was still a virgin back in high school. Really—scout's honor.

We returned to New York, and we did see each other occasionally for movie and dinner dates, but I finally realized why Henry would be a lifelong bachelor. Another sad story.

I'm glad I was wise enough to get out when I did because I found out through Google searching Henry a few years ago, that he went to prison in the late nineties for stealing money from his legal clients in patent scams. Go figure; I'm glad I went with my instincts back in 1981.

Each time I went back to the *candy store*, Mack Sabatino asked me, "What happened?"

I just said, "Mack, you've got to find me a *normal* guy." Though, for quite some time I had begun to think that maybe it was I who wasn't normal. Of course, I know *now* that I'm *not* normal, and I wouldn't want to be. What defines *normal*, anyway? However, as I look back so many years, perhaps I was giving off signs of desperation. After all, I was twenty-seven and never married. Back then, most girls had been married by then, had one or two kids, and some had already been divorced.

"Fanny," said Mack. "How'd you like to take a look at this guy? Let me tell you a little about him." Joseph Feinman was recently divorced, thirty-one, with no kids, and was a research scientist. Five feet, eight inches, with curly, light brown hair and a mustache (duh…by now Mack knew about my facial hair fetish). Not particularly tall, but tall enough. I watched his videotape and he gave off a lost soul image, so I figured he might be fair game for Fanny's company.

Joe lived in Dobbs Ferry in a small, one-bedroom apartment in a private house. He was born in Queens and had a master's degree from SUNY Albany. He had worked for RUB Environmental in White Plains for the past six years. That's a good sign, I thought. So, "Enough of his background," I told Mack. "Tell him to come in and view my tape."

Joe said yes to Mack. In the fall of 1981, we had our first date. Joe picked me up in his ancient silver 1964 Chevy Nova convertible. Well, enough for impressing a girl with a late model car, I thought. I was used to dating guys with Cadillacs, yet something about Joe intrigued me. Maybe it was the way he didn't exactly look me in the eyes when he spoke. He looked over my head and spoke to my hairstyle. Strange.

I found out that in addition to being a science aficionado, Joe loved to tinker with Chevys—the older the better. On our way to Rudy's Beau Rivage, a fine restaurant in Dobbs Ferry, Joe spoke about his ex-wife, Julie, and the reason why they were divorced. Julie decided she didn't want children and Joe most definitely did. Hmm…a good sign, I thought. After all, David said I would eventually want kids, though I still wasn't feeling any particular maternal instinct yet. I told him about my job in Harrison and how much I enjoyed the import-export business.

We ordered the *soup du jour*, which was a thick and wonderful beef noodle soup topped with garlic butter croutons. It was so filling that we had little room for the crab entrée salads, so we asked the waiter to pack them in take-out containers. We both enjoyed the classical background music which clearly enhanced the atmosphere of the lovely landmark restaurant. Then, back in the old Nova with the leaky ragtop whistling in the wind, we took the scenic way along Route 9, up through Irvington, then Tarrytown on our way back east via 287 to my apartment in Port Chester.

There definitely was a mutual attraction, but this time I knew I did not want to rush things. I had learned many lessons. It was about eleven p.m. on Saturday night and I had to get up early Sunday morning for an aerobic dance marathon in Mamaroneck. I had been actively participating in Jacki Sorensen's Aerobic Dancing since 1979 and loved the workout as well as the skimpy, neon workout clothes all the girls wore. After a few kisses, Joe asked if he could spend the night, which I thought was a bit odd, but I confessed to having an early morning workout appointment the following day.

I immediately thought he had a bet with his roommate, Will, that Joe could convince me to spend the night. I knew if he stayed over there would be no way I'd be able to get up at 5:30 a.m. to be fully awake, bathed, with breakfast consumed, and be down to Mamaroneck by 7:30 a.m. for rehearsals. Otherwise, were it not for that dance marathon, I might have let Joe win that bet. Before he said good night, he asked me out for the following Saturday night.

twelve

The Second-Date Proposal

I did a little dieting the past few days in preparation for my upcoming brisket orgy. You see, Freddy told me the PR folks at FUC had arranged for the third-generation owner of the most popular kosher-style deli in history to pay a visit to our show today, which would have the theme of common Jewish deli meats. Remember the scene from *When Harry Met Sally* where Meg Ryan's character celebrates "the big O" at another famous New York deli? "I'll have what she's having." Well, that's exactly how I feel whenever I have brisket. Maybe I should wear a Depends just in case?

"Viewers, today is a special day on *Fressing with Fanny*. Get your pickles ready for a debauchery of deli meats. Please welcome our guest, *Schmecky* (slang for little penis) Liebman, owner of the Eat Me Deli on Delancey Street."

In walks our rotund, bald guest with bushy eyebrows the color of a black and white cookie he surely sells at his celebrated restaurant. "It's S-H-E-C-K-Y, woman! Not the Yiddish equivalent of a male member. My parents, Izzy and Ida Liebman, named me after their favorite comedian, Shecky Greene."

I make some excuse about being so excited about the brisket and he forgives me. We move over to the counter where Puff and Duni-B have just set up four steam trays. We have a few cutting boards to accommodate the large roasts and an array of deli mustard, Russian dressing, cole slaw, and pickles. Half sour for me and kosher dills for everyone else. Fresh, thickly-cut rye bread slices make the display picture perfect. Lavender platters await the forthcoming masterpieces.

Like a skilled artist painting a picture, Shecky begins to hand-slice the pastrami, corned beef, brisket—be still, my heart—and last, the tongue, placing several slices of each in sections on the platter. A work of art.

I commend Shecky on his aptitude and grab a few slices of rye bread. I take a *Fanny* plate and plop a dollop of Russian on each side of the bread. Then I lunge for the brisket like a bitch in heat. One big bite and I'm about to fall down. I look for my stool and place my *tuchas* down, munching and sighing happily at the creation.

Shecky turns to look at me and asks, "What, no tongue? We have the finest tongue in the world!"

To which I reply, with a mouthful of brisket—not even taking time to swallow, "No *dahlink*, my Solly has the finest tongue in the world." Cut.

Though I couldn't put my finger on it, for some reason I felt excited about my upcoming second date with Joe Feinman. At work, I told Missy the bookkeeper about my new date and the wise older woman with two grown sons merely offered, "Take it easy." While I really liked Missy and felt she was way more maternal than my own mother, I was still a know-it-all and would have to find things out for myself for quite a few years yet to come.

Joe picked me up and we drove to the old Ground Round in Mamaroneck. They were known for their tasty, inexpensive steak dinners. Those were the days when there were peanut shells and popcorn all over the floor and you filled up on them before they delivered your entrees. So you almost always had to take a doggie bag. Eventually, they stopped the freebies, I think, because first, it was unsanitary, and second, they most likely had fat and happy rodents running around having a field day after the evening crowds left the premises.

I liked that Joe wore the top three buttons open on his button-down dress shirts so I could stare at his light-brown chest hair. He looked over the top of my head and said, "You really should wear a bra because I don't like other guys staring at you." My perky little B-cups stood up well on their own. I wasn't thrilled with being given an order, but I did start wearing a bra after that even though I hadn't worn a bra for the previous five years. After all, I thought, it takes two to tango in a relationship. Maybe I was learning?

Dinner was fun and we returned with our doggie bags to my apartment where we smoked a joint and then turned on channel four at 11:30 p.m. for *Saturday Night Live*. Feeling a slight buzz and mellowing out a bit, I observed how Joe grew excited when the space alien Coneheads family came on for their comedy scene. He laughed so hard I thought he would choke. We commenced to fooling around and, as they say, one thing led to another. We fell asleep in each other's arms and fortunately, in those days, I was able to sleep through Joe's earthquake-like snoring—an affliction that has befallen many a Jewish man. Could it be the shape of the Ashkenazic male jawbone?

I had a dream that night about a hairy caveman in outer space. When I woke up, I never would have thought how prophetic that dream would be. But we'll get into that much later on.

Joe started to stir and then said in a mumble, "Good morning, Fanny. Oh, by the way, if I get you a ring will you stop seeing other guys?" Now that I look back, the way he phrased that made him seem a little insecure. And weren't there supposed to be fireworks ablaze in the night skies when one pops the question?

Clearly, something was missing here, but in an effort to avoid OMS (old maid syndrome), I said with equal enthusiasm, "I guess so."

What kind of proposal was that? Was that, in fact, a *real* proposal? I was excited, *I thought*. But to ask someone to get engaged just so she wouldn't date other guys?

However, I felt even more weirded out when Joe tiptoed from the bedroom to the bathroom, his naked caveman body covered with light brown hair all over, and silhouetted by the early morning light, he proceeded to take a bath. Remember, I didn't have a real shower—just a shower hose. You see, after I told him where to find a towel, all of a sudden I started hearing the strangest sounds. "...*Space Cowboy...Rocket Maaaaaan...Ground Control...*" Just as Joe finished singing one set of off-key lyrics to each of three space-related mega songs, he looped the same phrases over and over again, almost ritual-like, until his bathing routine was done. Where the hell were my earplugs when I needed them, I thought. So, the mystery was, why would he sing Steve Miller's "The Joker (Space Cowboy)," Elton John's "Rocket Man," and David Bowie's "Space Oddity" in the shower?

Well, I pondered, at least he was clean. *Oy vey.*

Joe suggested we take a ride down to Katz's Deli on Jerome Avenue in the Bronx for a nice brunch. At that time I'd lived in the Bronx all my life up until five years before and had never been there. Joe had lived nearby on Mosholu Parkway when he was married to Julie, so he knew Katz's well. We drove west on 287, over to 87 South, exited on East 233rd, and then drove west on Jerome Avenue to Katz's. It was quite the ten-foot-wide, hole-in-the-wall greasy spoon, but it smelled like heaven.

Joe introduced me to Mr. Katz himself, saying, "Meet Fanny, my fiancée." That would take some getting used to, I supposed. I shook his slippery paw and he began to hand-slice two corned beef sandwiches on rye.

I asked for Russian and I asked for a club roll, but he quickly said with a Yiddish accent, "*Ve ain't got no Rrrrushin. Only mustid—and no clob rrrrolls. Take it aw leave it.*" Quite arrogant he was, but the size of the crowds awaiting entry to that little hole in the wall substantiated the quality of the meats. Although he served brisket and pastrami as well, after many years of our visiting this establishment until Mr. Katz closed it in 1988 with a happy exodus to the Jewish promised land of Boca Raton, I learned that the melt-in-your-mouth corned beef was, by far, the specialty. As Ms. Streisand would say, it was "like buttah." While we were eating, I asked Joe, "So, what about the ring?"

"Oh yeah," said Joe as he looked over the top of my head. "I'll pick you up after work on Tuesday and we can go see a friend I have in Rockland County over the Tappan Zee. He's got a shop that's open late on Tuesday nights."

I think I got more excited over the ring than what it was supposed to symbolize. So, on Monday I told everyone at the office I was getting engaged. Both Mendel and Missy asked, almost simultaneously, "Are you sure? You just had your second date."

I smiled and said, "I think everything will be just fine." Hindsight is sixty-nine, uh, twenty-twenty.

So now I had a half-carat, oval-shaped diamond engagement ring in fourteen-karat yellow gold. I called my parents and told Mommy that we had to plan a wedding. They hadn't even met Joe yet—how could they since we'd only had two dates? But they knew me well and didn't even bother to ask questions. They just said, "Mazel tov," probably rolling their eyes like they always did when faced with my unconventional escapades. Of course, I couldn't see for sure over the phone. We spoke about a June 1982 wedding.

Now that I look back, I only wish they'd asked if I really loved him. Love was never factored into the equation. Getting married was what gals my age, twenty-seven, did back then. Love would be a perk—a by-product—if you were lucky. But was this going to be a Jane and Michael Goldman-type, loveless marriage? Would I be going the same route my parents did? Only time would tell.

In a few weeks, Joe would plan to move out of his apartment in Dobbs Ferry and move in with me in my little old flat in Port Chester. The following Saturday night, Joe came over and I made dinner. Saturday nights would be the same routine. Either dinner or movie or both, then *Saturday Night Live*, then Joe's explosive laughter at the Coneheads, then a little mattress surfing, then the "Space Cowboy," "Rocket Man," and "Space Oddity" serenade during bath time. I finally got up enough nerve to ask him why he sang the space trilogy during every bath and he simply replied, "Because I really like those songs." Well, okay then. I would eventually find out the real answer.

thirteen

Living on Auto-Pilot in Rye Brook

By now you're aware that, for a long time, I've kept strange hours because of my insomnia. Freddy, Myrna, and Bobby have been kind enough to accommodate my odd schedule by filming afternoons instead of mornings. Fortunately, none of them were morning people, so that was a lucky break. I started keeping weird hours when I opened up my business years ago working online with factories in China. More on that later. Since they're twelve hours ahead over there, I used to begin working at nine p.m. from my home office and it would be nine a.m. the following morning in China, just as the office workers were beginning their days. I'd often not get to bed before three a.m. and probably not fall asleep before five. To this day, bright morning sunlight is hard on my eyes.

So last Friday evening, I had a brief meeting with *the girls*, Myrna and Bobby. Myrna said they had some good news and some bad. They were able to get Andy Chang for next week's show (good), but he only filmed mornings (bad).

"We need you to get here by nine a.m. on Monday," said Bobby.

I thought quickly and then said, "No problem; put me up at the Morehead Hotel around the corner Sunday night and I should be okay."

What possessed me to think that just because I was staying at the Morehead Hotel and I'd be an hour or so closer to the studios on Monday morning, I could party like a college frat boy on Sunday night? Then keep my normal hours, go to bed at five a.m. (thanks again, Solly, you animal), get up at 7:30 a.m., and still be bright-eyed and bushy-tailed for my show's famous guest?

Andy Chang, star of the PBS food show series *Big China*, had been around almost as long as Julia Child. Tall and thin with a gray crew cut and wrinkly face, Andy still spoke with a heavy Chinese accent even though he's lived in the USA for over forty years. *Big China* has been a PBS hit for at least twenty-five years.

"Friends, it is my honor—yawwwnn—to present to you today's special guest, Andy Chang, though this man needs no introduction. Many of you have grown up—yawwwnn—with his series, *Big China*."

Andy walked in like a tall penguin, swaying from side to side—kind of like the main character in the old silent Charlie Chaplin movies. "Andy, you remind me of Charlie Chaplin," I said, thinking that would be a compliment. Growing up, I'd always loved the funny silent movie character dressed in a black suit and top hat and the way he teetered side to side when he walked with a cane hooked on his arm.

Instead, Andy started screaming at me in Chinese, which by his facial expressions made it seem like he was cursing me out. The only thing I understood was "Charlie Chan," even though I had worked with Chinese factories since 1990, so you'd think I'd have known more. Especially since I'm somewhat of a linguist. I started to crack up, but Andy looked like he was about to strangle me.

"Wait, Andy, calm down. Did you say 'Charlie Chan'?" I asked. For those of you younger than fifty, Charlie Chan was a fictional Chinese detective in several popular movies in the 1930s and 1940s, as well as a 1950s TV series, played by heavily made up American actors who were supposed to look Chinese. This became a controversial topic for racial stereotypes and bigotry many years ago and, of course, if you know me by now, I would have no part of that.

"Andy, I said 'Charlie Chaplin', the fine English actor, not 'Charlie Chan', the fictional character." Andy finally calmed down and I think I saw a smile, even though he got pissed off again because I was leaning against the counter and yawning.

"Why you yawning? You bored?" asked Andy, sounding really insulted.

"No," I said. "Solly and I had a college frat party last night." Now he really looked confused.

So we proceeded to talk about the dish of the day, kosher-style *Egg Foo Young*. No pork, no shrimp. Andy reminded us that this was a Chinese-American dish that was rarely served in mainland China—usually only in Chinese-American restaurants. I said that many of our viewers liked the vegetarian version with just mushrooms, onions, celery, and scallions, to which Andy shouted, "YOU PEOPLE don't eat no pork, no shrimp? These are two best ingredient for dish!"

"Don't say 'you people.' That's disrespectful to many of our viewers who are Jewish. Are you getting back at me because you thought I said 'Charlie Chan'?" Yawwnn. It was becoming a zoo here between the yelling and my yawning. But all of a sudden, as we got to frying the onions and mushrooms, the scent from heaven calmed both of us down and we orchestrated the rest of the segment like a perfect food symphony.

With the *Egg Foo Young* plated, I offered Andy a fork and a glass of white wine. "*L'chaim!*" said Andy while clicking his glass against mine. I was dumbfounded as to where he picked up this Yiddish toast.

"Oh, by the way," said Andy. "Open up envelope." He handed me an envelope with two tickets to the SAMMY Awards. "Make sure you come!"

We eventually went out to Queens so I could meet Joe's parents. They were thrilled that their son would be getting married again. They lived in a high-rise building in Rego Park. Charlie and Rachel Feinman were a cute couple in their sixties, and like good Jews, for them it was also all about the food. Rachel didn't do much cooking, although when she did, she packed a mighty punch.

Both were second generation Jewish New Yorkers who kept a kosher home. However, whenever we visited out came the paper plates and plastic flatware and we'd have a bountiful *treyf* feast from the nearby Chinese restaurant in Forest Hills. Tung Sing was famous for its savory *Egg Foo Young*. Rachel would call in the order and spend about half an hour on the phone with the restaurant. First, because she had to speak slowly so Hung Lo could understand her, and second, because the order was so huge it filled the back of the restaurant's old Woody station wagon.

I had to admit after trying it, Tung Sing's *Egg Foo Young* was the most delicious I had ever eaten. Not greasy at all, chock full of onions, mushrooms, celery, and—for those who wanted it—tasty bits of either roast pork or shrimp, both taboo if served on anything other than paper plates in the Feinman home. And every time we visited, the four of us would always eat until we were about to explode. Both Charlie and Rachel were chubby, though even after dinner and on a full stomach, Charlie would go around cleaning everyone's plate, eating whatever little bits of food were left. Rachel often scolded him but I thought he was a cute old guy; and, his behavior was typical of a child of the Depression.

On Saturdays during daytime hours, I was free to go out shopping (what else?) while Joe tinkered with his old Nova in good weather. On Sundays we'd go down to Katz's on Jerome, then either visit my parents in the Bronx, or head to Queens to visit Joe's folks.

Next on the agenda was to find a rabbi, as neither of us belonged to a temple. We asked around and Mendel at work recommended Temple Shalom in Scarsdale, a Reform congregation. That was also good because, while we both liked the traditions and culture of Judaism, neither of us was particularly religious. We just needed a way to make it legal.

I bought a vintage lace midi-length white dress by Gunne Sax—no way was I going to wear a bridal gown—and I dressed it up with a wide, lavender (of course) satin ribbon at the waist. A few weeks before the wedding, I got my very first perm, as the eighties were big for big hair, and mine had been thin and pin-straight all my life. It was time for a change. I ordered a lavender and white basket bouquet for me, lavender silk flowers for my hair, and a pink and white bouquet for Cami, whom I asked to be my matron of honor. I was the maid of honor at her wedding three years before. She was now pregnant with her first child, so she had to find a special dress; maternity dresses back then were not particularly fancy.

June 20, 1982. We had a small gathering of family only at Temple Shalom, though, of course, a few of my most intimate co-workers insisted on attending the ceremony as well. As Rabbi Moskowitz pronounced us husband and wife, Joe stepped on the glass, kissed his second bride, and thus began our life together. At twenty-seven, I was "Sadie, Sadie—Married Lady." We had a small luncheon—also for family only—at the Red Cabin in White Plains while an unsolicited aging hippie woman serenaded us to Noel Paul Stookey's "The Wedding Song (There Is Love)" accompanied by her guitar. She was actually quite good. Thirty-some-odd years later, I'm still trying to figure out where the hell she came from. We asked the restaurant manager and even he was clueless.

It was off to Disneyland in Anaheim, California, a week later for our honeymoon. Joe was able to schedule a business trip to one of RUB's satellite offices in Buena Park, California, so at least part of our expenses were covered. Although between the two of us we both made decent salaries for that time of economic prosperity, Joe didn't like to spend money so I sort of followed suit and adapted to his lifestyle—all the while I silently questioned it. I kept thinking, it's our honeymoon…let's live it up. With him, the more he made, the more he'd want to stash under the mattress. Hence, twenty-year-old cars and a cheap honeymoon. I could never understand that.

The one thing that I do remember clearly was how excited he became when we rode Space Mountain. I didn't make a connection then, but instead of seeing the entire Disneyland park, Joe insisted on waiting on line to ride Space Mountain fourteen times that day. So, when asked where we went for our honeymoon, I just said, "To Space Mountain."

Meanwhile, within a year or two, my old 1973 Dodge Dart Swinger bit the dust. After all, it was over ten years old and even in its better days, it only got about eight miles per gallon. It had a huge, rusted-out hole in the floorboard under the driver's seat, so in cold weather, I froze in places on my body that were always normally quite warm, if you please.

Joe insisted we go to a car dealer all the way in Langhorne, Pennsylvania, even though he was against my buying a new car. He said this place was where his dad would always go for cars, and would successfully *handel* (barter with, in a negative Jewish-stereotypical manner) the owners. This just wasn't my nature, so I let Joe take care of matters, but I insisted on a new maroon 1983 Ford Escort. It made me wonder, though, if it was worth *schlepping* that far when we didn't even take the time to comparison-shop locally. Penny wise and pound foolish? No matter, Fanny. Joe's cost-cutting became a predictable pattern.

We left my old Dart there in Langhorne, got temporary plates, and I followed Joe's trusty old Nova on the highway back home to Westchester County. It wasn't until summertime, however, that I realized the reason for the $6,249 *great deal* we got on the car was because it had no fucking air conditioning.

Joe and I started to look at houses and condos in 1983. We found a tiny old house in Rye. It was around the corner from the beach, which would have made me very happy for many years. I was always a flip-flops kind of gal. But we eventually settled on a two-bedroom, two-bath cooperative apartment in Rye Brook, which again, for some reason, Joe managed to put in his name only. Red flag? Seriously.

I became pregnant in early 1984. David Tobin was right; I'd eventually want kids. Maybe I was ready to replace the one I chose to lose?

At the end of March, we moved from *my* cold and drafty third-floor little walk-up in Port Chester to *Joe's* co-op apartment (not mine) in a majestic old luxury building in a neighborhood of more of the same grand old luxury buildings in Rye Brook. The only difference, I thought, among the structures were the names, written prominently on elaborate plaques in front of the properties, such as "Provincial Arms," "Brook Terrace," and "Blue Pond Cooperatives" which was the sign outside of our building. Other than that, if it was dark and you couldn't see the signs, you could easily walk into the wrong building. I got to park on the street and, of course, Joe got the one-per-apartment indoor parking space.

I really didn't want to leave my old, drafty apartment that was *my* home for over four years. Something made me stop and think…could I *schlep* a baby *and* a baby stroller up and down three flights of stairs every day if I stayed there? At least it was mine. Daycare? I'd figure that one out. But Joe was scary when he gave ultimatums: "You're coming with me. That's my baby too." I was such a wuss.

So, equipped with four migrant workers from a street corner in the rough section of Port Chester who spoke no English and came from a country I'd never heard of, Joe rented a $19.99 U-Haul special. He then commandeered what he made sure to tell me was the best deal he'd ever made on a planned relocation.

The new building's lobby was quite elegant, with several chandeliers in the center of the seriously lofty ceilings. The mirrors all around the perimeter made the entryway look double its size. It was impressive, I guess—more than a few steps up from my parents' 696-square-foot little old house in the Bronx. And quite the bargain for Joe, priced at just $50,000—easily worth double—but I later found out he bought it at an estate sale. The previous owner had kicked the bucket a few years before and it became a burden for the doctor son to maintain. He just wanted out.

So by now you must be wondering why I never confronted Joe on matters I felt might have been unfair or odd, such as his *handeling* ways and my not being treated like an equal partner. Or, the way he would insist on stopping *everything*, no matter the time of day, to watch any of the scheduled NASA space flights. Goddess forbid if he were at work and couldn't watch. You know for sure that he'd take advantage of our new VCR, tape the flight, and watch it the second he arrived home from work without stopping to greet me—I always got home first—or come to the table for dinner. He just sat mesmerized and paralyzed in his rust-colored velour recliner in front of the TV and appeared like he was about to climax, just as the spacecraft was launched.

I guess, although you'd never know it now (Fanny don't take no shit!),

I was just old school back then. Although Mommy and Daddy had a loveless marriage, despite Daddy's repeated attempts to be affectionate towards Mommy, she clearly made it known she wanted no part of it.

Now that I have my beloved Solly, that all seems so foreign to me. But with Joe, I was just coasting along, living with blinders on, grateful not to be an old maid. I was working five days a week at a job I enjoyed and watching my growing belly with a little boy or girl hiccupping and dancing inside me. Besides, all good Jewish girls should be married, right? Sheesh… It would take more than a dozen years before I embarked on a path that would show me what I'd been missing.

In the summer of 1984, I used to sun and swim in the plush, green courtyard's little outdoor pool with my one maternity bathing suit. One Saturday afternoon, a pretty blonde *shikse* sat down on the chaise next to me and introduced herself. She was petite and had a beautiful figure.

"I'm Lizzie, what's your name?" she said as she extended her hand. I introduced myself and even though I really wanted to be left alone to work on my tan, Lizzie was the sweetest thing. She lived in the adjacent building (three buildings shared the pool) and had just had a baby girl.

She immediately said, "You know, I have so many maternity clothes; I bet you could use some." I looked at her and back at myself and saw that I had a good thirty to forty pounds on her, and probably at least three to four inches in height.

No matter. She insisted I come up for a visit to see her new baby and take a look at the clothes. Lizzie, a *goy* (Gentile, non-Jew)—I guessed right—was married to a Jewish chiropractor who had offices in Mamaroneck and was a nurse before she had little Macy. Lizzie's kindness was infectious and we became fast friends. Lizzie had a nanny, so we could go shopping or hang out as often as we wanted.

Now I had some new, very tight maternity clothes, most of which I never wore except for a really pretty red blouson maternity bathing suit, which probably started out being at least three sizes too big for Lizzie, luckily for me.

I worked at Chemical Commodities full time up until the day I went into labor. Joe and I had taken Lamaze birthing lessons at the old United Hospital in Port Chester since all my doctors were affiliated there.

My kind office mates were all concerned for me as it was just a few days before I was due. A few of us went to the Ground Round in Mamaroneck for lunch and I decided I'd have a full Mexican platter, beans included, against the wishes of my companions. They were worried such spicy, heavy food, especially the refried beans, might bring about my first child right then and there at lunch. Well, they weren't *too* far off, and I was more than ready…

fourteen

Fanny at the SAMMYs

Solly and I waited for the limo to get us and I started to get nervous due to Duni-B's and Puff's giggling around the set whenever they'd walk by me this past week. Maybe they knew something I didn't? Whenever they giggled, funny things happened—like the time Duni-B's mother, at the age of forty-six, went into labor with Duni-B's baby sister, Vera-B, also named after yet another leading handbag and accessories company. This got me thinking about my two babies who were no longer babies.

My Lori, at thirty, is a lovely, poised young woman, savvy and stylish. She's engaged to Paul, a sweet, smart, and talented technician for Ford Motor Company. And my second baby, Mitchell, at twenty-six, is involved in research and academia and will be completing his PhD in a few years. He'll be marrying Josh soon and Solly and I can't wait to attend our first gay wedding. We're sure it will be just *fabulous*.

The limo company texted us to say they'd be arriving at 6:30 p.m., which I hoped would allow enough time to get us from here in central New Jersey to Radio City Music Hall by 7:45 p.m., the time we were instructed to arrive.

Solly saw I was getting really nervous, so he whipped out a blunt and said to me, "*Mameleh*, take a couple of hits so you can relax." We weren't driving, so we both had more than a couple of hits. If we had more time, Solly and I might have headed to our boudoir to release some tension. Solly's nickname is the "Eveready Bunny," but instead we stumbled out the front door. Solly grabbed my ass as I walked in front of him in my long, sequined purple gown, and my shiny silver flip-flops. He looked so handsome in his penguin suit that I, in turn, grabbed something else once we were seated in the rear of the long, white limo. And with the dark-tinted windows, only Solly, the limo driver, and I were privy to the activities en route.

Traffic was building up at the Lincoln Tunnel but we didn't give a shit. We arrived, still buzzed, just in time for me to stop and take a quick glance at the marquee outside that stately old theatre. "Welcome to FUC's SAMMY Awards."

Andy Chang, with his grating accent, was serving as master of ceremonies. *Oy vey*; who the hell was this guy screwing? He was all over the place. I would have thought they might have gotten another celebrity for emcee, maybe like Pamela Dunn, the controversial Southern belle kitchen master. But her accent can at times be equally as grating. After all, Andy had yet another book coming out— his thirtieth in twenty-five years—so it was then and there I realized I must get moving with mine. As we were seated, Solly once again put his hand on my ass, patted it, and said, "Fanny, just chill. I suspect that today is *your* day."

There were awards for the best Southern cooking, the best Ethiopian cooking (get real,) the best Mexican cooking, and the best barbecue shows. About midway during the ceremonies, Andy introduced Freddy Giordano, Myrna Klein, and Barbra (Bobby) Fleishman as producers at the Feed Us Channel. Andy had a tough time enunciating their names. It sounded more like he was reading dishes off a Chinese take-out menu.

Freddy walked out, a tall and gorgeous Burt Reynolds clone, with Myrna, thin and gangly in red (of course) to his left, and a stout Bobby in a ladies tux to his right. He began. "This one was easy. All of you viewers voted for our next winner. And if you knew the circumstances under which this show came about—uh, let's just say I met this woman over thirty-five years ago, when for me, she was the star of the Mamaroneck Motel." Then I heard, "Allow me to present the SAMMY Award for Best New Show to Fanny Goldman, star of *Fressing with Fanny!*"

I was just sitting there dreaming I was in an alternate universe, realizing this must have been some potent reefer, watching good-looking Freddy speak, when Solly stood up, gave me his hand, and escorted me right up to the stage. As if awakening from a reverie, I realized I was on stage, standing with my three inimitable bosses in back of me.

I immediately took the mic, put my hands up to "shhh" everyone from applauding, and began. "Such an honor, a *mechaya* (a pleasure; orgasmic), a *brocheh* (blessing)," and I proceeded to rattle off in Yiddish, even though I wasn't in any way fluent. Then I continued, "*Muchas gracias a mis hijos, a Solly y a toda mi familia del FUC* (Many thanks to my children, to Solly, and to my family at FUC)." Where the hell did *that* come from? I guess Spanish came more naturally to me than Yiddish since I'd been speaking *that* since 1965.

The diverse audience proceeded to applaud and Freddy grabbed the mic to quickly add, straight-faced, "I guess next year we'll have to hire a translator."

The four of us began to leave the stage to laughs, then applause, with Myrna and Bobby taking the lead. I was holding the heavy, gold-plated, sandwich-shaped award. As we reached the backstage section, in a tricky, unlit area Freddy muttered something about wanting to take me to the Mamaroneck Motel. I thought to myself, that's odd. First, he was married. Second, I was about to be married to my Solly. And third, I didn't even know if the motel was still in business. The way he mumbled, it seemed like he was actually thinking it might have been 1978 again. He had a strange look on his face.

Meanwhile, although I was caught off guard, I told him, "Why don't you let Tina take you home and you two can make believe you're at the Mamaroneck Motel tonight?" He just smiled with a bit of a blank expression on his face. Of course, I wouldn't say anything to Solly because it wasn't necessary. Nothing happened. I'd just have to make a note to myself to watch out for anything else that might seem odd…

So I sat back down and Solly gave me a warm peck on the cheek, which made me want to peck his pecker. Then we enjoyed the rest of the show, even though with Andy's annoying voice I felt like listening to something on iTunes on my phone if only I'd had my headphones with me. I had to stay there to support my fellow FUC fans and celebrities. I quickly took a selfie of Solly and me with my SAMMY, posted it online, then group texted Lori, Paul, Mitchell, and Josh to share the good news with them.

Amid congratulatory texts, Mitchell asked, "Fanny, are you stoned again?" How on earth my son could pick that up on a phone is beyond me. But he's always been talented and intuitive.

I remembered when he was eighteen, the summer after he'd graduated from high school. He confessed to me he'd been smoking both pot and cigarettes since he was fifteen. I wasn't shocked, as even I was able to obtain my stash from some of the parents in his Flower, New York, school district. Fortunately, neither Lori nor Mitchell had ever had a problem with substance abuse, though, with their unusual pre-teen years, you'd have thought that might have happened.

By ten p.m. Andy thanked everyone and I thanked goddess he was finished. I must admit, it was quite a trip both attending such a fancy live awards ceremony *and* being given an actual award at the same ceremony. I'd attended awards ceremonies many times over the years and had even won an inventions industry-related award, but nothing nearly as cool as an award for being the star of my own FUC show.

On the limo ride back home, Solly called me his very own star. We saw the limo driver look in his rearview mirror and roll his eyes. He was a handsome African-American fellow of about thirty, but then I thought I heard him mutter something under his breath like, "Fucking old people should just get a room." He then smiled, closed the partition, and said, "Aw, go for it. Knock yourselves out."

Once home, Solly and I realized we had a really bad case of the munchies, especially since we thought a dinner might have been involved as part of the night. After all, it was a food-related awards show. Dumb idea, because where can you put tables inside the stately old Radio City Music Hall with all those rows of seats other than perhaps on the stage? Duh.

No matter; Solly to the rescue. He rushed to our spacious kitchen, pulled out a bag of Brach's Chocolate Stars, quickly microwaved some movie theatre-style, heavily-buttered popcorn, added some raw almonds, and tossed everything, with the popcorn still hot, into a big bowl. Some of the chocolate melted and it was one seriously delicious concoction. Solly said while passing me the bowl, "Stars for my star." Damn, I love this guy!

fifteen

And Babies Make Four

*O*y, *mameleh*. What a memorable night. Now, *the girls* told me there'd be press conferences, magazine stories, *social media blasts*. What the hell was that? I really must get used to this new technology. And, I'd have to do more work on my book *"ASAP"* as Freddy told Mandiyee to tell me. With my brain running a thousand miles per hour, I was getting hungry. Matter of fact, I began to crave my *Masterpiece Meat Loaf.* I proceeded to text Solly to pick up three pounds of good quality ground beef on his way home. I liked big meat. I was certain I'd have all the other ingredients at home.

That night back in 1984, after I'd had such a heavy Mexican meal with my co-workers at the Ground Round, I started having some intense Braxton-Hicks contractions. Because this was my first birth, I had no way of knowing how long it would take for these to become *real* contractions. I asked Joe to take me to the hospital late on the evening of October 22. The nurses examined me and said I had quite a while to go. They wanted to send me home, but Fanny wasn't going anywhere.

I officially checked in just after midnight on October 23. I labored for forty-five and a half hours and I had to hand it to Joe. He clocked the contractions and stayed by me the entire time. A few times I asked for morphine and Demerol because I was never one to handle pain well and I hadn't slept at all in almost two days. I knew nothing about epidurals, which could have saved me a ton of grief. During the final stages of labor, I requested an old-fashioned method which I'd heard could be a last resort...an enema. I learned that during the transition phase of labor, a woman can lose all inhibitions—that is, if she even had any to begin with. So there I sat facing backward on the hospital toilet because I had intense back labor and got rid of my Mexican dinner from two days prior. Note to preggo women in labor reading this: go the Mexican-enema route!

When my gyno (female, of course) said it was time to sit on the birthing chair, I practically did a jig in between contractions. I don't know if they still use birthing chairs, but I think whoever designed them was a genius because they really helped your anatomy do its job as gravity helped to pull the baby downward at a perfect angle. After a few heavy-duty pushes, although I clearly indicated on my admission documents that I would refuse an episiotomy, I yelled down at the doctor's head between my legs to, "Cut me, goddammit!" And she gladly complied as she wanted to get home to her family after almost two days.

On October 24, 1984, at 9:36 p.m., a golden-haired little star, Lori Guinevere Feinman, made her appearance. Her middle name came from a song by David Crosby that Joe and I really loved. She weighed six pounds, ten ounces, and the next morning as I held her near the window, I noticed she had wisps of gold throughout her reddish blonde peach fuzz. Joe was beside himself and Lori would forever become Daddy's little girl. I just kept on thinking, as I held her, how could such a perfect, pretty little human come from *me*?

The hospital food sucked, so I asked Joe to bring me a brisket sandwich, with Russian and cole slaw, on a club roll from the Rye Ridge Deli the next day. I'm glad I had some cash with me because I had to pay for it.

I was able to stay in the hospital for four days and was grateful because I had no experience with babies. The staff taught us how to bathe and feed

Lori. They even sent a nurse to check on us a few days after we'd gotten home, courtesy of United Hospital. Back then, medical insurance was so much better.

Fanny on a soapbox here: nowadays, with a vaginal birth you're lucky if they let you stay overnight. I miss the old days of good, cheap health insurance, with little or no co-pays.

Six weeks after I got home from the hospital, and with Joe and me taking turns bottle feeding Lori round the clock, we were both exhausted. I chose not to nurse. We finally called Senior Personnel Agency and hired a wonderful baby nurse named Katrina who was able to get Lori on a four-hour feeding schedule. By the time she was seven weeks old, Lori slept through the night. We had put a cot in Lori's room and Katrina shared it with her, so we really had no idea what went on behind closed doors. Katrina was born in Berlin in 1920 and lived there through the war, so Joe and I jokingly thought she might have used military tactics on little Lori to get her to sleep. But in reality, Katrina, a spinster who never had children, was just a natural with babies. When she spoke to Lori in German, Lori's eyes opened up wide and she smiled.

The days breezed by and after four months I went back to Chemical Commodities, but on a part-time basis. I had the best of both worlds: Lori, my precious little beauty, and an income. I was fortunate to take so much time off because a typical maternity leave was just six weeks. We hired a local babysitter three days a week named Del, whose responsibility was to take care of Lori and clean the house while Lori napped. Cheap help was hard to keep and we later had another babysitter who robbed us while Joe and I went out one evening. She was supposed to be watching Lori, but instead, she opened the house up to her undocumented family members.

It wasn't until after we came home, paid the woman, and sent her on her way that we realized all of the Hanukkah presents that were wrapped and stored in our bedroom closet were gone. Yet another babysitter, Shel, either drank Lori's baby Tylenol or doped Lori up so she could take frequent naps because I noticed the empty bottles each time I went to replace them. You're out. We didn't like her anyway because she used to go out on our terrace for a smoke, also when the baby napped, so she always reeked of cigarettes.

After a while, we found an older Italian-American woman who was quite the grandmother figure. And, since Lori was little and still took naps, Lena had time on her hands and loved to cook. So we had dinner awaiting us the three days a week I was at the office. She would give me a shopping list for the week and the fresh tomatoes, basil, and chopped meat were all the makings for an unforgettable pasta sauce, spaghetti, and the occasional meat balls or meat loaf. She left me handwritten recipes, which on occasion I would modify from Italian-style to Jewish-style, usually by removing the parmesan, oregano, or basil depending on my mood or cravings. Meat loaf became another of my signature dishes. Lena lasted the longest of our babysitters, until the time when Lori started pre-school and I adjusted my work schedule around Lori's school days.

In mid-January 1987, as soon as I arrived at work, Mendel told me to turn around and head down to the Bronx. He wouldn't tell me why, and of course, we didn't have cell phones so I couldn't easily contact Joe, who I figured was on his way to work too. Whatever was going on, my sixth sense told me it wasn't good.

When I arrived, I saw my brothers, Marty and Harry, sitting on the couch next to Mommy, holding her hands, just as Joe arrived. I learned that Daddy woke up to go to the bathroom around eight a.m., returned to the bedroom, fell backward, and died in bed. He was only sixty-seven, poor guy, with a quack of a primary care doctor who never properly treated Daddy's diabetes.

Mommy looked ashen because although she supposedly "hated" him, she was married to him for over forty years, so now what would she do? Within a few minutes, a local funeral home director carried Daddy out in a body bag. I was numb but more concerned that Lori would never see her Pop-Pop again with whom she adored singing old songs and coloring with crayons. She was his baby girl's baby girl. Insert sad face emoticon here.

When Lori was a little past three, I started having serious sinus issues, so Joe recommended an ear, nose, and throat specialist in White Plains. The diagnosis was a deviated septum which could be easily fixed, so I was told, by sinus surgery. I was never one for elective surgery, but Dr. Esterman assured me he knew what he was doing. No healthgrades.com existed in 1987.

We brought Lori down to Grammy Jane's in the Bronx, I had my surgery at the old Saint Agnes Hospital in White Plains, and remembered awakening with a crucifix over my bed. Had I known, I would have asked for a Star of David. A few days afterward, when the swelling went down a bit, I realized that one of my nostrils had sealed shut, so I could not breathe through that nostril. Dr. Esterman, who said, "Wow, this has never happened before," suggested waiting six weeks and then he would go back in if the nostril hadn't opened up by that time. Sure, he knew what he was doing.

And it didn't, so I had surgery again. The good thing was, I was finally able to breathe. But the bad thing was that having surgery again so soon caused me to have constant, mind-numbing pain in the sinus area between my eyes. I continued to work three days a week, but after a while, I couldn't take it any longer.

While I loved my job and co-workers (and my financial independence from Joe because I had my own spending money), I had to give notice and then go on painkillers while looking at possibly suing Dr. Esterman for malpractice. Joe and I interviewed a few lawyers, but no one wanted to touch the case because back then, you actually had to prove malicious intent.

During the summer of 1987, I was watching a country music trivia game show on The Nashville Network which was a precursor to Country Music Television. It was hosted by Whisperin' Bill Anderson, a famous country singer and songwriter, and called *Fandango*. Joe sat fascinated as I would answer each trivia question correctly, even before the TV contestants had a chance to hit the buzzer. So Joe said, "Why don't you try out for the show?" Of course, I'd have to go to Nashville, and who would take care of Lori?

First things first: they advertised auditions by phone and I passed with flying colors after just five questions. I was scheduled to film in December, so Joe suggested I bring Mommy with us and she could watch Lori while I was at the studio. Now, Mommy hadn't been on a plane since World War II, but she happily consented. Daddy had passed earlier that year, and she could use the company. And Mommy was neither negative nor depressing when little Lori was present.

The three of us flew to Nashville where I rented a car and we stayed at a nearby luxury hotel on Elm Hill Pike. We had a blast attending tapings of many of the TNN shows with famous country music celebrities. And on one of the days I wasn't filming, we took Lori on a riverboat cruise even though it was December. It was cold but the boat had a heated inside cabin where everyone huddled. Lori, at just three years old, asked the guitar player if she could sing a song and he most happily handed her the mic. She blasted out Roger Miller's "King of The Road" while the picker strummed his guitar. That was one of the songs I'd taught her while singing with her on the white rocking chair in her room every night before she'd go to bed. It was our little ritual. After everyone applauded, she had the biggest shit-eating grin.

On the day of filming the show, it was so cool being glammed by studio make-up artists. The sets were elaborate, with neon lights everywhere. I had a few changes of clothing with me because they filmed several shows each day. I would be playing against two other contestants. I made sure to have an Inderal with me because my doctor said it would help the stage fright I knew I'd experience. This was in addition to the painkillers to which I'd become accustomed for the sinus agony.

In walked Whisperin' Bill, a friendly, gentle giant, who shook hands with each of the three contestants. I was the only Yankee there that day on the show, and would you believe, even though I was competing against southerners who'd grown up with country music all their lives, I won the show.

A few crappy prizes, such as a 1987-modern telephone answering machine, desk calculator, exercise bicycle, and a case of Liquid Plumr, would be sent to me in New York a few weeks later, along with an autographed photo of Bill. Of course, when I got back home, Joe said he wanted to try to sell the prizes because he thought he could get back some of the gift taxes we'd need to pay at the end of the year. Again, we didn't need the money, but money—and outer space—were his obsessions.

I went backstage and changed my clothes for the second taping, but a gal named Phyllis from Louisville, Kentucky, massacred me almost immediately. She had the nerve to say to me, *"Yankees cain't know nuthin' about no country music anyway."* Except that I won the first show, lady. Besides, by that point, several hours later in the day, I'm sure the Inderal was wearing off, so I was losing that winning edge.

After I finally figured out what she had said to me with her thick, redneck Southern accent, I looked her in the face with a big smile and said, *"Shtupp-es in hinten, zoyne* (Stick it in your ass, you whore)." She smiled back with a puzzled look on her Walmart-lady face.

Still, it was a memorable trip for me, for Mommy—who enjoyed the *Grand Ole' Opry* show on an outing by herself one of the nights that Lori was tired—and for Lori, the budding riverboat country music artist.

I remained in touch with my friends at my old job, many of whom I'd known for the almost eight years I'd worked there. There must have been some sort of divine intervention in my leaving because a few months afterward, Chemical Commodities was bought out by a British firm and the Harrison, New York, office was closed. Some of my co-workers were let go, while some went to work in the New York City offices.

Was it also by divine intervention that I noticed I didn't need my evening painkiller that would help me to fall asleep? Yes, insomnia's long been a part of my life. I also started feeling a bit nauseated and missed my period. I was like clockwork and we really weren't planning on having more children, at least perhaps for a few years. Especially since Lori was a handful. She had been speaking her mind, in full sentences, since she was twelve months old. I went to my gyno who confirmed my suspicions. Yes, I was pregnant, and sometimes pain such as the type I'd had from the sinus surgery-gone-wrong can go away with pregnancy hormones.

Of course, Joe was thrilled, our families were thrilled, and I was just thrilled that I had no more agonizing sinus pain. As I look back now, as a busy soon-to-be mom of two, I rarely took the time to stop and smell the roses which I make it my business to do every day now that I'm older. I had to learn to be grateful, *the hard way*, and I'll tell you about that soon enough.

I immediately felt fatigued and would take a nap when Lori was in pre-school and another as soon as Joe came home from work, before dinner. Certain foods made me turn away (yes, even Fanny turned away from food during pregnancy), so I lived on a lot of applesauce and bland foods until at least my third trimester.

And now that I didn't have my own income, I was miserable because Joe gave me just a small allowance each month from which I'd have to purchase groceries and whatever I'd need for myself and Lori.

As I grew bigger, everyone, including myself, thought I was having another girl. Everyone except Mommy. Jane Goldman had a special old-world talent for correctly predicting the gender of a baby in-utero. She was never wrong and she said I'd be having a boy. I thought I'd wanted another girl. But on December 9, 1988, Mitchell Reuben Feinman, at six pounds, twelve ounces, entered this world at 5:58 a.m., after just five short hours of intense back labor—and yes, the enema worked again. As he was passing through the birth canal, I began to have a feeling that it was a boy. A mother's intuition, but I was overjoyed.

Since he had a full head of pitch black hair, Joe and I thought he probably inherited the Goldman genes because Joe's side all had light brown hair. Mitchell looked just like a cute baby monkey. Mommy, who was watching Lori in the Bronx, brought Lori by for a visit at the hospital to meet her baby brother. Lori beamed as she got to hold him while sitting in her Grammy's lap. And Grammy Jane began to call him her "Butchie" immediately, a nickname that stuck with him until she passed, a little over twelve years later.

Soon after Mitchell was born, Joe told me as he looked at my hairline, never straight in the eyes, "Now that I have a son, you won't ever have to work anymore." What, was Lori chopped liver? And how about upping my allowance for *two* kids now? That did not happen, but money was never the real issue.

Now there were four of us and Mitchell never slept.

sixteen

One Big, Sort of Happy Family

After the SAMMYs, one of FUC's outsourced IT specialists, Ravi Patel, assigned me a *Kvetcher* (person who complains or whines) account and I quickly had to learn how to *kvetch* (to complain or whine). So I was on the phone with him and who the hell knew what time it was there in India? It sounded like he was having a hard time staying awake, but he had to coach me through this uncharted territory as I told him to slow the fuck down and stop singing a song. Not that I hadn't been *kvetching* all of my life anyway, but this was a little different. *Oy*, social media.

First, I had to pick a password, so I thought, why not E-A-T-M-E? But I finally understood enough of Ravi's sing-song to learn that it had to be at least eight characters. So it became E-A-T-M-E-N-O-W. That would be easy enough for me to remember. All I have to do is think of pillow talk with Solly.

Now I had to figure out how to post about the show, my SAMMY award, interesting Jewish-style recipes, and other tidbits. My kids told me that for *Kvetcher* each post must be two-hundred characters or less. No one has ever been successful in limiting Fanny Goldman before, so it was going to be a challenge for me to be cut off. *Oy*.

Here was my first *kvetch*, and I hoped *the girls* would be satisfied: "Sincere thanks to all the fans of *Fressing with Fanny* for the SAMMY for Best New Show. I'm working on a recipe book for all of you Fanny fans but Solly says I'm running out of characters. HELP!"

Whenever I get nervous, I cook. Maybe a nice carrot raisin salad with walnuts. I've always had carrots, golden raisins, and walnuts in my kitchen. And how my kids used to love golden raisins—"reenies" as they called them. They were so cute when they were little…

This time we had the experience to know that newborns do not sleep when you need to sleep. Joe would have to go back to work after a week or so. And now with two little ones and sleeping never being a talent for me to begin with, we decided to retain a baby nurse for at least a week or two when I came home from the hospital with Mitchell. We kept in touch with Katrina, our first baby nurse with Lori, but she was unavailable.

Mrs. Neeley was a full-figured African-American woman with dark eyes and a pageboy haircut, who always wore a white uniform. Everything about her was big, even her hands. She was almost able to fit tiny Mitchell in the palm of her hand. But she was gentle and loving with him, especially when we had his *bris* (ritual circumcision ceremony given to Jewish baby boys when they are eight days old) because I had no idea how to care for a circumcision wound. And, we had to wait until Mitchell was nine days old—a Sunday—because the eighth day, when a bris is typically held, fell on *Shabbos* and of course, you can't do anything on the Sabbath.

We assembled the immediate family in Queens at Joe's parents' condo. They hired a skinny, old, white-bearded *mohel* (person who performs the ritual Jewish circumcision) and provided a delicious dairy brunch for those who attended. The scent of the abundant spread of bagels, lox, cream cheese, whitefish, and all sorts of salads wafted in the halls of the building as the guests entered. The halls of all Jewish apartment buildings smell the same.

Soon, the rabbi did his deed. Tiny Mitchell, sucking obliviously on a Manischewitz-soaked ball of gauze, wearing an equally tiny light blue and silver crocheted *kippah* (religious circle-shaped head covering), made a quick shriek. Then the *mohel* diapered him swiftly and deftly, wrapped him up in a blanket and handed him immediately to Mrs. Neeley who stopped his whimpering with a pacifier. A harmony of *mazel tovs* and then began the mass exodus to the dining room to do what Jews do best…eat. Predictably, one by one, the guests began to describe the foods in front of us as though they were a religious experience—a gastronomical orgasm.

"This cream cheese is as light as a cloud. So heavenly."

"I've never seen lox cut so thinly."

"*Oy*, this tastes just like my *Tante* (Aunt) Sylvia's pickles. I must get the caterer's recipe." These were all among the many reviews from the amateur food critics.

Back home, thankfully, Mrs. Neeley tended to baby Mitchell's wound and I actually slept a few nights while she was still in our employ. After two weeks, Joe and I were left to take care of our two delightful wee ones: a four-year-old verbal little miss and a newborn who wanted to stay awake all the time, perhaps thinking he'd miss something if he slept.

For months, I would take a nap when Joe would come home from work and then by midnight I'd be up most of the night tending to Mitchell while Joe slept so he could go to work at seven the next morning.

Before Mitchell was born, Joe and the building super had built a little nursery for Mitchell, cutting off part of the living room, which was oversized anyway. So now we had an almost-three-bedroom condo. We really didn't want to put a newborn in with Lori anyway. Katrina, Lori's former baby nurse with whom we remained friendly over the years, came for a visit for a few weeks. She declared Mitchell as one of the first babies in her long career who gave her a challenge in the night sleeping department.

By the time Mitchell was six months old, every night by about four a.m., once he gave his last, "Hey, come and entertain me," notification and I was sure he was safe and dry, I would turn off the baby monitor. We only had an audio monitor; baby monitors with cameras hadn't been invented yet. I knew he'd be okay for two or three hours until we'd start our routine all over again in the morning. I'd walk into his room in the morning and there he was in his crib with a big toothless smile, happier than a pig in shit, carrying on a conversation with Lulu, his plush bear. Was I a bad mommy? I don't think so. He was fine. Lori was a talented sleeper and Mitchell was not. And way back then was when *my* talent for sleeping began to decline even further.

In addition to not being a good sleeper, Mitchell was a fussy eater, whereas Lori ate everything. She particularly loved lobster and shrimp and would beg for it in restaurants until we found out she was allergic to shellfish as a pre-teen. Maybe she was haunted by a distant deceased relative trying to remind her to be kosher? Remember, shellfish is taboo for us Jews. It's not like I give a shit, though.

Mitchell, on the other hand, would live only on four-ounce jars of ready-made Gerber baby oatmeal with apples. He ate jar after jar intermingled with the occasional banana and sippy cup with milk. Boy, was I ever grateful for those Flintstones vitamins.

So, in April 1990, the "now that I have a son, you won't have to work anymore" grew old. After all, Joe had more than once told me he felt that I should substantiate my existence. What exactly would you call taking care of a household and two young children? I grew tired of having to ask for money, which was certainly not lacking. Research scientists made a comfortable living. It was time to find daycare for Mitchell and a part-time job for Fanny. Of course, I'd have to take the cost of the daycare out of *my* salary, but at least I'd have a salary.

I read the newspaper and found a classified ad for a part-time import job. That sounded terrific, especially since the firm was only a mile from our home. I had imported for about fifteen years by then, so I had lots of experience. I called and made an appointment for an interview and then quickly typed up my résumé, which hadn't been touched since 1987 when I left Chemical Commodities in Harrison.

I had been out of the workforce playing the role of "Fanny Mommy" for a few years, so I had no interview clothes. Because it was only a local part-time job, I borrowed a nice tunic top and plain trousers from Mommy and walked in confidently to Land-Ocean Imports in Rye Brook. No business suit needed there. I aced the interview and began the job as part-time import assistant the following week.

Mitchell was sixteen months old and an active, curious toddler who couldn't get enough of *Sesame Street*. Lori was in kindergarten and although she had two long blonde pigtails, she loved wearing her Dorothy Gayle blue and white gingham *Wizard of Oz* dress made famous by brown-pigtailed Judy Garland. Both children enjoyed our nightly ritual of reading *Berenstain Bears* books together.

Within the week remaining to prepare for my new job, Joe and I decided that we'd try to find a home-based daycare to coincide with my part-time work schedule, which also worked around Lori's school schedule. From an ad in the local newspaper, we interviewed Olivia who was a schoolteacher in her native country, Argentina. Her home looked warm and clean and she had anywhere from three to six children there on any given day. Her references were good, and she was less than one mile away from my new job.

Olivia spoke mostly Spanish with some English and Yiddish intermingled. Most of her charges were children of local Hispanic migrant workers so Mitchell became bilingual in Spanish and English as a toddler learning to speak. This was an asset that carried him through college while living abroad in Salamanca, Spain, as well as when he was chosen as the valedictorian of the Spanish department for graduation from Fordham University many years later. And, since Lori was already learning a little Spanish in kindergarten, I often spoke in Spanish to both of them. We were a multilingual household between English, Spanish, and the occasional Yiddish expressions from our parents.

I enjoyed the privilege of working three days per week as well as the two days per week I was able to spend with both children after Lori came home from school. After a few weeks at the job, Lauren and Malcolm Silverman—the Jewish owners of the firm—called me into their offices to say that the import manager, to whom I reported, had given two weeks' notice. Would I like to take over Ruth's position? Of course, they knew I had two small children and had chosen to work just three days per week, but they would try to work around my schedule. They were kind and generous people and after consenting, I offered to bring paperwork home if necessary. They trusted my abilities and were pleased with my experience and professionalism.

So in less than one month of employment, I was promoted to import manager of a long-established international sporting goods firm. I was a little nervous because I only had two weeks for Ruth to train me before she left, and although the principals of importing are the same, every business has its own style of record keeping. And this was before computers helped simplify procedures. At times I was lost and when I would ask the president, Malcolm, how best to solve a problem, the old sage would always say, "Figure it out." Those three words gave me the confidence to get through many times of turmoil in years to come when I would really have to figure things out. Most of those times were with my choices in men.

I began to get used to being a working mom. And the financial independence wasn't shabby either. Soon, after only a few months of employment, I got a considerable raise which turned my part-time hours into almost full-time income.

Mitchell was still a picky eater, so rather than forcing him to eat Olivia's daily *fideos* (noodles) and lunch meat, he was proud to carry his little *Teenage Mutant Ninja Turtles* lunchbox filled with snacks or peanut butter and jelly sandwiches and juice boxes with him the days I was working.

By the time Mitchell was four, he used to beg for those little three-ounce cans of Chicken of the Sea—"chickie," as he called it. He would eat the entire can using his colorful plastic toddler forks practically every day for dinner in our little eat-in kitchen. Then, his loving eight-year-old sister decided she'd heard enough of "chickie" so she told him, "Mitchell, that's tuna fish, not chicken." He threw the fork and can in the sink, spat the remaining contents from his mouth (also into the sink), and started to cry.

"I won't eat fishies." I had no idea where that came from. But if he's anything like his mother who doesn't eat poultry, I guess it's hereditary. And although both he and Josh, his fiancé, are gourmands, Mitchell still won't eat anything that swims.

Up until he went away to college, his limited dietary range left him with pizza, chicken nuggets, hot dogs, and juice boxes as his only daily menu options. Oh, and yes, the occasional butter-grilled cheese sandwiches, only when Grammy Jane made them. As colorfully and enticingly as I would try to prepare raw veggies or fruit salad, Lori happily munched away, while Mitchell turned his head and either didn't eat or waited for the next meal.

Thankfully, they were both healthy, though one would think Mitchell might have had a cholesterol problem with that diet. Both kids did like to nosh on what they called "reenies," or raisins, in little zip-lock plastic snack bags. Over the years, I accumulated a back seat and floor full of those little buggers when I removed the car seats to junk my silver 1990 Hyundai when its engine died.

As time flew by, Joe and I really didn't spend much time together as a couple. On weekends in nice weather, he would have his Saturdays free to tinker with his collection of twenty-year-old cars in the co-op's outdoor parking lot, while blasting "Rocket Man," "Space Cowboy (The Joker)," or "Space Oddity" cassettes on his car radio. Aside from the one indoor space which Joe claimed, each apartment had one reserved outdoor parking space. Joe knew all of the seniors who didn't drive, so their parking spaces became his for all of his old cars.

I would take Lori and Mitchell to the Bronx to visit their Grammy and the four of us would go to flea markets, shopping, or movies chosen by the children. On Sundays, Joe would take them to visit his parents for Tung Sing take-out in Queens and I would spend the day at the beach or shopping with my good friend from work, Milagros, who was the controller at Land-Ocean Imports.

Milagros joined the company a few months after I started working there and we became fast friends. She was about eighteen years older than I and was born in Cuba. She soon became the big sister I never had and we liked to speak Spanish to each other if we didn't want anyone else knowing what we were talking about. Her children were grown and she had recently divorced. She was the type of person with whom you felt comfortable sharing your darkest secrets—and I was destined to have plenty.

On long holiday weekends when both Joe and I were off from work and school was closed, we would occasionally travel to Bucks County in Pennsylvania for sightseeing, shopping, and Sesame Place, a fun outdoor amusement park for kids. I loved the flea markets. Once, we went with Joe's parents and took three adjoining hotel rooms for two nights. Our favorite buffet-style restaurant there was Old Home Buffet where kids' meals were ten cents times their ages. And kids four and under ate for free. So, for example, when Mitchell was four, and Lori was eight, we only had to pay eighty cents for her meal and the costs of the adults' meals, which were also reasonable. The food at the buffet was always fresh, clean, and appealing to the eye.

When it was time for dinner, Joe decided to stay back at the hotel to tinker with his old car, which always needed some sort of part, so just his parents, Lori, Mitchell, and I headed out to the buffet. Just as we were hooking Mitchell into his car seat, Joe ran out after me and handed me a plastic Tupperware container just big enough to fit into my tote bag. I often used tote bags as there was always something I'd need to *schlep* for the kids like a snack or spare t-shirt or crayons.

"Here, take this and bring me back some food," Joe said while looking over my head. "And make sure you don't pay for it." Now, you have to remember that Fanny *then* was not the same Fanny *now*, so I did whatever Joe told me to do. I just thought it was odd because it's not like we couldn't afford the cost of one more dinner.

When we arrived at the restaurant, we found a nice, big table for the five of us. I took the kids up to the buffet to select whatever they wanted before I got my plate. After Charlie and Rachel sat down with Lori and Mitchell to eat, I went up, filled two plates, and came back to the table. I began to eat while placing the second plate underneath the table, rushing to shovel it into Joe's Tupperware container.

Almost immediately, a manager, along with one of his servers, quietly came over to me and said, "Either put the food you took back on the table or pay for it." Joe's parents just looked at each other and shrugged their shoulders as they knew their son. I was so embarrassed—not so much for myself, but for the kids. I apologized and put the plate on top of the table.

In addition to the shame of being a bad example for my children by way of their father, I had to go back to the hotel and explain why Joe would have to go out for a burger after working on his car all day. And Charlie made sure to run around to adjacent tables before they were bussed to pick at the leftover food after the dining families had left as Rachel tried to get him to stop. His child-of-the-Depression mentality prohibited him from wasting food, even if it was food discarded by strangers.

seventeen

Disney World, and...

I was so excited to hear that *Abuelita* (Grandma) Lolita, star of FUC's *Mi cocina es mi vida* (My Kitchen Is My Life) was coming to cook with me on my show. After Google searching her, I learned she used to be a teenage cook and housekeeper for a wealthy Jewish family in Cuba before Castro pulled a number on the innocent citizens in the early sixties. I was happy to hear she spoke a little Yiddish in addition to, of course, Spanish as well as English, but with a heavy accent. I thought, terrific, all bases are covered for me because I'll be able to understand her. However, I'd never heard anyone speak Yiddish with a Spanish accent, so this would be a first.

"Friends, I'm so pleased to welcome the popular chef, *Abuelita* Lolita, star of our network's *Mi cocina es mi vida*." Lolita is a petite woman of no more than five feet with shiny gray hair wrapped in a bun to reveal an aged face with penciled-in black eyebrows and porcelain skin. She was surely a beauty in her prime and looks to be in her early seventies.

"*Abuelita*, I bet you were one hell of a Lolita back in the day," I say. She gives me a puzzled look but stands next to me and I talk about the recipe of the day, my *Colorful Corn and Black Bean Salad* with lime and red peppers. I drain a package of thawed black beans along with a package of thawed yellow corn.

Lolita dumps the corn and the black beans into a mixing bowl and I ask her to dice the red peppers while I rub the lime on the tabletop with the palm of my hand to release the juices before I cut it in half.

"Lolita, after you add the diced red peppers, please add a *bissel zalts* (a little salt) and then I'll add the lime juice."

Lolita smiled at me and said, "*¿Quieres que ponga un poquito de sal* (you want me to add a little salt)?"

To which I immediately replied, "*Sí, por favor* (Yes, please)." It was clear we were a trilingual duo and we totally understood each other. I was just hoping the viewers, the majority of whom spoke just English, caught on to what we were saying.

Next, Lolita said, with her endearing thick accent, "Ju no put cilantro and red *cebollas* (onions)?"

To which I replied, "No, *mi amor* (my love). I'm allergic to cilantro and red onions make me burp and my breath stink." I don't know many Jewish dishes that use cilantro, anyway. She just laughed and continued to stir the mixture in the bowl.

We each grabbed a tablespoon, dug in, and clicked our spoons together while Lolita said, "*L'chaim*," and I said, "*A su salud* (to your health)." It was delicious.

After the segment, Lolita pulled me aside and asked me, "Why dis Frrreddy he tell me I look hot? Whas rrrong wee heem? Dat no nice. He acting like he a teenayer? He no married?"

I just looked at her and said, "*Oy vey*. He's been saying the same to me, too, and yes, he is married. I'm beginning to worry about him because he's always been a perfect gentleman." I'm going to watch Freddy, but think I'll soon have to have a talk with his wife, Tina.

Summer of 1995: Joe and I wanted to take the children to Disney World. Now that Lori was ten and Mitchell was six, we figured they'd be the perfect ages to enjoy the whole experience. Ever since he was small, Mitchell has always been obsessed with airplanes and airlines. By the time he was six, he knew every model of every airplane of every airline that flew throughout the world as well as the number of seats and windows in each plane. He knew the routes, connections, hubs, and ultimately declared that he wanted to be a commercial pilot when he grew up. Not a shabby aspiration if you ask this Jewish mother.

Now Mitchell and Lori would get to fly to Orlando and this would be Mitchell's first time on a plane. As you know, Lori came with Mommy and me to Nashville in 1987 but she probably was too small to remember much of that trip.

We flew Kiwi Airlines out of LaGuardia and Mitchell was ecstatic. Before we arrived at the airport, he told me we'd be flying on a 727. And how did a six-year-old little boy know this? It was then I began to see a similarity between Joe's fixation with the "Rocket Man-Space Cowboy-Space Oddity" songs and Mitchell's obsession with airplanes and flying. Of course, I was no scientist, but I thought there had to be some sort of strange genetic component with those two similar fascinations. But now was no time to analyze, Fanny. Just sit back and enjoy the trip, I thought.

When the flight attendants turned off the seat belt warning lights, you can be sure Mitchell asked Lori to walk him up to the cockpit so he could ask the pilots to have a look. Back then, prior to 9/11, pilots and flight attendants were happy to accommodate a small child's wishes. Mitchell and Lori got to see all the pilots' equipment and even got a little set of wings to pin on their shirts. This is something Mitchell still talks about.

In Orlando, we rented a car and drove to the International Drive area where we stayed at one of the La Quinta properties. Everything seemed to be painted in bright yellow throughout the hotel and the grounds. Each morning, while Joe wandered the local garage sales and junkyards for car parts (yes, even on vacation), the children would swim in the pool as I sat in a lounge chair poolside and enjoyed the Florida sunshine. This has become a lifelong passion for me and one day I will become a snowbird with a small property in Boca Raton. Solly has already given me the green light for this and we will start searching in a few years.

On Wednesday morning of the five days we were down in Florida, we rode the hotel's shuttle to Disney World. We had pre-purchased the Disney tickets at the hotel for a discount, of course. The minute we walked through those welcoming gates, Lori and Mitchell ran to shake hands with Mickey and Minnie. I made sure both had plenty of sunscreen and hats to protect them from the peak sun hours. Lori had a sweet pink baseball cap and Mitchell's was blue with a little Mickey Mouse on the brim.

The long walk down Main Street was crowded with families and little kids darting in and out of the store fronts. We stopped at an old-time photo store where we dressed up as a pioneer family straight out of the nineteenth century. The black and white photo looked quite authentic.

Soon it was lunch time, and of course, Mitchell wanted chicken nuggets. Lori was much more easy-going with her lunch selections. So we had to hunt down a place that sold chicken nuggets while Joe complained that, "At these prices, we should have packed a cooler with lunch for the four of us." How often would we be taking the family to Disney World, so why couldn't we just buy a lunch there? What was the big deal?

We walked through Fantasyland and the kids ran from ride to ride. Wouldn't you know it? Joe left the three of us so he could go back and forth on Space Mountain for almost the duration of our visit. I kind of expected this. It was a déjà vu from 1982 at Disneyland in California during our honeymoon. So I just took the kids on rides I knew they'd like and for which we wouldn't have to wait too long in line. It was mid-week, so Disney World wasn't too crowded. We did the Haunted Mansion and the three of us enjoyed It's a Small World and Pirates of the Caribbean.

It was adorable to see Lori and Mitchell singing It's a Small World for the rest of our time at the park. Joe met us later at around 7:30 p.m. at Cinderella's castle and he proudly announced he'd ridden Space Mountain about ten times. We had dinner at a nearby kiosk and because he was fresh from his Space Mountain fix, he did not complain about the food cost. You had to know how to play the man. We waited for the Main Street Parade and then came the nine p.m. spectacular fireworks.

Both children fell asleep in the shuttle on the way back to the hotel and it was a memorable day for my two little Disney characters.

When we returned to New York, both Lori and Mitchell had plenty of stories to relate to their teachers about their trip and I'd have tons of pictures to share with Milagros and friends at my job. Of course, I'd have to wait a few days until I got the film developed.

In October 1995, Joe had to take a trip to New Orleans for his job over the long Columbus Day weekend. I thought, gee, it's been quite a long time since we'd been away together, *just the two of us*, so I suggested I'd go with him. Because his company was paying his expenses, I'd just have to pay for my airfare and meals, of course. It had been quite a while since Joe had treated me to a meal, let alone a trip. But I had never seen New Orleans and Milagros, as controller and HR manager, was more than happy to accommodate my part-time schedule at work, especially since we were such good friends. We arranged for Joe's parents to watch Lori and Mitchell. It was a long weekend and school was closed anyway. They were happy to spend time with *Bubbe* and Pop-Pop in Queens since they saw Grammy Jane in the Bronx almost every weekend.

We flew into New Orleans and stayed at a luxury Hyatt. I stayed at the hotel reading, listening to country music on the radio, and relaxing while Joe had meetings during the day on Friday. He had one more meeting on Saturday morning and then we were free to check out the French Quarter in the evening. We found a small Creole place called Paulie Chic's which had some spicy shrimp and rice dishes. On Sunday, we took a drive to the casinos in Gulfport and Biloxi, Mississippi, which were just becoming popular back then. We stayed overnight at a Motel 6 near the casinos, then drove back to New Orleans on Monday morning so we could prepare for our flight back home.

On the flight back to New York, Joe shared some unexpected news with me. Or was it really? "Fanny," he said while looking at the hairline above my forehead. "I've seen an attorney and filed papers to change my name from Joseph Feinman to SpaceCowboy Feinman."

I guess I must have been coasting along in this marriage with blinders for the past thirteen years, but I never saw this one coming. For me, I couldn't give a shit if he called himself "Dickhead," because I'd kept the name Fanny Goldman throughout our marriage. Never once did I call myself Fanny Feinman.
But what about the kids? Sure, they knew he sang those cosmic songs during his daily showers, but it was what they were accustomed to. That was just part of their daddy's charm. However, how would they explain to teachers and friends that their daddy, Joe, was now SpaceCowboy Feinman? Although they were still very young now, wouldn't it be slightly odd when they were teenagers? *Oy vey.*

eighteen

OMG...

I was logged on to my *Kvetcher* account at the studio. I'm still getting used to this social media shit. Maybe you *can* teach old Fanny new tricks? I was about to *kvetch* my two-hundred or fewer characters when Freddy knocked on my door.

"How ya doin' Fanny doll?" I smiled, motioned for him to come in, and told him that all was quiet on this front.

"So, how's by you?" I said. He grinned and asked about my cookbook. They wanted to start advertising it, maybe even plan a book tour. I told him I should be done shortly and that I was finishing up one of the last recipes.

Freddy said, "Tell me about the recipe." But then he started to close his eyes as if in a trance. He looked like he was falling asleep, then opened his eyes and said, "When can we go back to the Hotel Hershey again? We had such a great time last week, especially with that melted chocolate bar."

Now I was really worried. That was over thirty-five years ago. What was happening to him? He's not that old...sixty-five? I quickly grabbed his arm and walked him back to his office where Mandiyee was coming around the bend looking for him, thankfully. By the time he was back in his high-backed leather chair, he seemed more grounded.

I raced back to my office/dressing room and put a note on my phone to call Tina. There have been too many odd things coming out of the Guido Adonis' *moyl* (mouth) lately. Most of the time he was sharp, but more often he was slipping back into 1978.

I grabbed my iPad, and began my *kvetch*: "OMG! You won't believe all the recipes Solly and I've been testing recently at home. You'll soon be the beneficiary of such deliciousness, but we must finish soon before we gain too much weight."

SpaceCowboy decided to take the two children into the living room and tell them that he'd changed his name in case anyone at school asked about him. To them, he'd always be "Daddy," so they really didn't care and they were too little to understand the eccentricity of this action.

In early November 1995, SpaceCowboy told us he had to hurry and schedule a business trip to Tampa, Florida, where RUB Environmental had another satellite office. That company was all over the map. Mitchell, Lori, and I drove him to LaGuardia Airport on a Saturday morning and he said he would try to be back within a week or two, tops. While he was away, he would call in the evenings to speak to Lori and Mitchell before we'd read our *Berenstain Bears* stories at bedtime.

The kids and I picked SpaceCowboy up at the airport the following Saturday. He told the kids about the lovely weather and that, "I accomplished what I needed to down in Tampa." But while he was speaking, he had a strange look in his eyes. Not that I wasn't used to his peculiarity, but something this time was different.

Thanksgiving would be coming within a week or two, and for this year we'd be going to my brother Harry's and sister-in-law Karen's home in Yonkers to celebrate the holiday. On Monday evening, Harry called, SpaceCowboy picked up the phone, and Harry asked to speak with me.

"Fanny, just say yes or no to what I'm about to tell you. I imagine Joe is probably there in the room with you," said Harry. No one in my family would get used to the strange name change.

"Yes," I said.

"Do you remember David Tobin?" he asked as my heart jumped out of my chest while I made a monumental effort not to collapse.

"Yes."

"Just make it seem like we are talking about what you'll be cooking to bring with you for the holiday. But David remembered I lived in Yonkers and found my phone number. He called saying he knew you were married, didn't know your married name, but wanted to find out if you were happy. He asked if you had any children. I have his number, so if you call me at a time Joe's not around, I'll give it to you," said Harry. Everyone in my family had always liked David Tobin.

"Okay," I said. "We'll definitely bring the cranberry-orange relish and I'll make another side dish or a main dish for those like me who don't eat turkey." I almost choked, thinking I'd need a defibrillator within a few minutes. How on earth I even managed to spit *that* out was beyond me.

Fortunately, SpaceCowboy just went about his business helping to get the kids ready for bed. I don't know how I made it through the next day, but after work, I picked up the kids from school and drove to my friend Enid's home. I had gotten David's phone number from Harry earlier in the day. Enid's children were just about the same ages as Lori and Mitchell and went to the same schools. I told her that after thirteen years of coasting along in what was never a true partnership, I might have a chance to reunite with someone whom I'd loved with all my heart.

I quickly summarized the story of David Tobin and Enid, who had four children with two different husbands, smiled because she was always quite liberal in her views. She had to be in order to be a friend of mine. In the few years I'd known her, she'd dated a man from just about every ethnic group in every size, shape, and color. While our children were playing downstairs, she grabbed the phone, shoved it in my face and said, "Call now!" I ran to her upstairs bathroom and locked the door.

He was always young for his age. Would he be healthy? Was he still married? Where did he live? I began to think of all possible scenarios to stop myself from calling him, but here's the rub: David was David Tobin—first true love of my life—and SpaceCowboy was, well, Joe—father of my children, *period*. And strangely enough, it came to me then, clearly, that every night in bed with SpaceCowboy, I would dream about David Tobin. In my dreams, his son was already grown up. Maybe mid-twenties. And David had cute salt and pepper curly hair in the same mini-Afro style he'd always had, but shorter and more closely cropped. I would awaken and sadly recall that I hadn't heard from him in over fifteen years. Let's see, he'd probably be at least sixty-three by now. Who doesn't believe in ESP?

I began to tremble again, even though I'd never stopped shaking since the night before when Harry called. It's now or never, I thought. One ring and my life might be changed forever. A deep, resonant, and familiar, youthful-sounding voice appeared on the other line. "Hello?" And there he was, my beloved David, after all these years. This was a dream come true.

"It's Fanny!" I think that's when the expression "OMG" was uttered for the very first time, many years before texters and teenyboppers made it famous. "You sound like yesterday," I said, which sounded dumb after I thought about it, but I was sure David knew what I meant. With David, I could always be myself. The next words just flowed naturally from my mouth. "No one has ever been able to fill your shoes."

Then David said, "No one has ever been able to fill *your* shoes." I was beginning to feel comforted, safe, and warm all over, which were feelings I'd missed for so many years.

I asked him to tell me about his life, though I sensed it would take longer than the time I'd have for this phone call. First, David told me that he was a widower. His marriage lasted from 1980 to 1992 when Elsie died from an overdose of alcohol and prescription meds. David actually came home from work one day in 1992, right before he'd retired, to find her dead in bed. Then, I wondered, and the unfiltered-Fanny asked him, hypothetically, "Here it is 1995, so why did you wait three years to contact me?" Precious time lost for both of us.

David said he had a huge townhouse in Flower, New York, over the Tappan Zee Bridge, about an hour and a half drive from Rye Brook. He and Elsie bought it in 1987 and moved there from New Rochelle.

Our phone conversation continued for quite some time when I realized it was getting late and I'd need to take the children home for dinner. We both agreed to meet on Thursday, November 16, at nine a.m. in Elmsford, which was our old stomping ground in the late seventies. We both thought the Ramada would be a good place, *inside* the lobby, just in case anyone might see us out in broad daylight. As we were hanging up the phone, by force of habit, we both said, "I love you," at the same time, just like we did so many years ago. I was hoping no one would notice my teary eyes.

I ran over to Enid and told her I'd be meeting with David on November 16 and that I'd talk with her further as soon as I could regain my composure. I thanked her for helping to facilitate what I assumed would bring about indescribable forthcoming changes. She gave me a quick hug and winked at me, showing that she spoke the unwritten language of Ally-Woman.

I did my best to get through the ensuing days until I'd be seeing the man of my dreams. The next day at work was quite busy. While I was arranging shipments of sporting goods from China to worldwide distribution centers, Milagros was supervising the warehouse workers who were taking inventory. However, by then she'd been a good friend for over five years, so she asked me to spill the beans while she was passing my cubicle on her way to the kitchen to grab some coffee. She sensed something was different. I told her I couldn't talk, but asked if we could go to brunch on Sunday at the City Limits Diner in White Plains. Milagros and I both adored their *huevos rancheros*. Joe/SpaceCowboy would be in Queens visiting his parents with the kids, so this would be a perfect time.

Sunday, November 12: I brushed Lori's now light brown, shiny long hair and she chose a white printed top with pink fleece stretch pants and her favorite pair of pink jelly shoes. Mitchell, of course, chose his Pilot Mickey sweatshirt and jeans. Both looked adorable and picture-perfect in case *Bubbe* Rachel wanted to show them off to the neighbors in their condo building as she often did. A *bubbe's* privilege.

After SpaceCowboy/Joe left with the kids, I drove into White Plains at around eleven a.m. and found Milagros already sitting in a booth near the large, sunlit windows. About one second after I sat down, she said, "Okay, what's going on?" I suggested we order first because I'd need a long time to tell her everything. So we both ordered the *huevos rancheros*, mine with eggs over medium and no cilantro, Milagros' with sunny side up, and two coffees.

"You know how I always point to that old apartment I used to have in Port Chester whenever we go to eat at the Rye Ridge Deli?" I asked Milagros.

"Of course. Your eyes used to light up every time you spoke about David and how you loved living there with him," said my dear friend. "For some reason, I've never sensed that feeling with your husband. So, come on. I know you. Something's up."

"You'll never guess who I'm going to see next Thursday," I began. "David is still alive!" I told Milagros everything I knew, which wasn't too much, from the sole phone conversation I'd had with him last week. For fifteen years he was just a part of my recurring dream. My heart was doing a pitter-patter as I related the story.

Being the good Catholic girl she was, her first reaction was, "He'd better not be married."

I told her all about how he became a widower back in 1992, that he was retired, and that there was no way I *wasn't* going to meet with him in Elmsford while the kids were in school. After all, Milagros had always been aware of SpaceCowboy's/Joe's eccentricities because she was the only person I'd ever been able to talk to about my just-coasting-through-life feeling. She was the only one who would believe me when I told her about his recent name change. He was never nice to Milagros during family parties and seemed jealous of my friendship with her. Throughout our brunch conversation, I was convincing myself that meeting with David was my only choice.

Milagros simply smiled and said, "Go for it. Maybe you'll be happier, and ultimately your children will be happier. I'm sure they see no love between you and your husband."

We enjoyed our *huevos rancheros* and we each had three refills of coffee. Then we went to walk around the newly-opened, pristine Westchester Mall in downtown White Plains for the rest of the day. I had to find a top that was suitable for my "date" because I'd gained a few pounds and I was worried about my appearance. We both tried on several things and I ended up with a beautiful maroon figure-flattering tunic sweater and maroon plaid stretch pants with stirrups which were the rage at the time.

I drove Milagros back to her car at the diner and said, "*Te veo manaña* (I'll see you tomorrow)," because I'd be seeing her at the office on Monday. I squeezed her hand, which she has always taken to mean, *thanks for being there for me.* And I was there for her, a few years earlier, when she was going through her own divorce.

"Autopilot" was an expression that would best describe the next few days. Working Monday through Wednesday that week was the best distraction therapy this gal could ask for. It also helped for me to pick up my kids from school, go home, and cook them dinner. By then, SpaceCowboy/Joe was making his own weekly large roaster chickens because he was too busy to eat at the dinner table with the kids—he wanted to come home and read up on recent space travel news. As soon as he'd walk in the door, there was a perfunctory greeting, a hug for the kids, and then he headed straight to his La-Z-Boy in the living room with his *Outer Space Digest* or science fiction space book.

Lori, Mitchell, and I would enjoy our dinners in the eat-in kitchen, singing along to country music on the kitchen clock radio, and after we'd finished, I'd start their baths and get them ready for bed. SpaceCowboy/Joe would then go into the kitchen, take a portion of his Sunday-evening-made chicken, and nuke it for his dinner, sometimes with some potatoes or pasta I had left over in the fridge. But mostly we had an invisible line down the center of the fridge which separated his food from the goodies that the kids and I enjoyed. Was this normal? No. Was this a reality? Yes, and this was the only reality the children knew.

Fast forward to Thursday morning, November 16. I got the kids ready for school and threw on a pair of old jeans and a sweatshirt with my canvas slip-ons. For many years during my marriage, I never wore any makeup except for the occasional lipstick on special occasions. As I look back, this was clearly a reflection on my dull existence.

Lori and Mitchell finished off their bowls of Cheerios and orange juice and I drove them to school, a little over a mile away from home. After kisses and "Have a great day," I raced home and donned my new outfit, brown ballerina flats, and gold accessories. I tried to remember the best way to apply my eyeliner, shadow, mascara, and blush as my hands shook with excitement. A few minutes later, and I was 1980 (plus fifteen) Fanny again, plus a few pounds and this time with a curly perm instead of pin-straight long hair.

As I drove towards Elmsford, I nearly missed the exit on 287 because I was singing so loudly to Janie Fricke's song "She's Single Again" on the only country music station my car radio could pick up. It was light years before iPods and satellite radio. I swerved my car to the right lane, a foot short of side-swiping a green Chevy, exited onto Route 9A, and drove north to the Ramada. There was a parking space right in front of the lobby entrance. After checking my makeup in the rear-view mirror, I took a deep breath, closed my eyes, and whispered to myself, "It's now or never, Fanny."

As the automatic doors slid open to my destiny, there sitting on a chair right next to the front desk was my David Tobin. He stood and was still tall and thin at sixty-three with the salt and pepper closely-cropped Afro I'd seen in my dreams for the past fifteen years and the same mustache he'd always worn gracing his beautiful mouth. I ran into his arms and he kissed me right there in front of the hotel staff, who applauded. David must have clued the staff in to what was about to transpire.

"You look beautiful," were three words I hadn't heard in forever. I felt safe. I was home. I did smell tobacco, to which I was highly allergic, so I knew he'd gone back to smoking. But we'd talk about that later. Right now, I just couldn't let go. He suggested we go into the hotel's café for some coffee and breakfast, but quite frankly he could have said, "Let's go to Coney Island," and I would have followed him anywhere.

I couldn't eat; I was way too nervous. I ordered a blueberry muffin and tea but barely managed a few sips of the tea. I gave the muffin to David. It was not like Fanny to refuse food. I mentioned I'd gained a few pounds but David just said that I was way too skinny back in 1980. He knew exactly what to say. And with that, we both said, "Let's go upstairs." Each of us had reserved a room—I with an auto club discount, he with a senior discount—so we asked the front desk to cancel one. Hand in hand, we strolled to the elevator which took us to the third floor, room 325.

First, I told him all about Lori and Mitchell and how they were becoming such terrific little *mensches* (human beings) despite the lack of love between their daddy and me. Then I told him about SpaceCowboy/Joe. David's reaction was, "Geez, Fanny. Back when I told you to marry someone close to your own age, I really wanted you to fall in love. I was hoping for a caring, beautiful relationship for you." Oops. I'd failed. "But see, you do have two wonderful children. I knew you'd be a great mother."

Then he touched me like I hadn't been touched in fifteen years while I recalled all of David's old moves. All the right moves. Luther Ingram's "If Loving You is Wrong, I Don't Wanna Be Right" was playing on the room's clock radio. I had to have music wherever I went. Music kept me from going over the line. But this *was* right.

We knew we had to be together again. However, David was free and I was not. Realistically, we agreed, the only way we could be together would be for me to divorce SpaceCowboy and for David to marry me, as I needed medical benefits. There were no benefits for domestic partners back then and Land and Sea Imports did not offer medical benefits to part-timers. David had the cream of the crop IBM-retiree benefits. And, we were sure the children would need some sort of transitional psychological assistance.

For the second time, I had no down-on-one-knee "Will you marry me?" but this whole situation was far more romantic than any old marriage proposal. We were being practical. He had been a widower living alone for three years. I had been a married woman living "alone" for over thirteen years in the sense of a lack of true companionship. Now that would all change. I would have to figure out the right time to talk to SpaceCowboy about this. And I would ask the guidance counselors at the children's school to recommend a family therapist as the shit was about to go down, big-time. I wanted Lori and Mitchell to come through this as unscathed as possible.

There were many things to work on. I would be unable to call David from my home phone without SpaceCowboy analyzing and questioning the calls on the phone bill. He routinely did this to check for errors by the phone company. So for now, I'd have to reach David from work. David said he'd get me a cell phone as quickly as possible so I could call him any time for anything.

We made plans to meet again on Sunday, November 19. I'd first have to clear it with Milagros because she and I had a standing Sunday date every week while SpaceCowboy took the kids to Queens. After I'd told her my story, I thought, she'd be thrilled to give up one Sunday.

I'd meet up with David in Rockland County over the Tappan Zee Bridge at the Holidome. I would park my car there in the huge hotel lot and he'd drive me up to see his home in Flower, New York, north on Route 87 and west on 17. It was about an hour northwest of Rockland County. I would have just enough time to see his place, check it out for the children, and then get back home to Rye Brook before the crew would arrive back from Queens.

That day at the Ramada, we'd made a lot of plans and we both were exhausted. We took a brief nap and asked the front desk for a 1:30 p.m. wake-up call. I'd have to change clothes and remove my makeup to change back to the old, dull Fanny and head back to Rye Brook. I had all of these extras packed in anticipation in my trusty tote bag.

We held hands in broad daylight while David walked me to my car in the front. Now I didn't care if anyone saw us. The deal was sealed. A sweet kiss followed with, "I'll see you on Sunday at 10:30 a.m." I felt complete.

nineteen

Rocket Man, Literally

I'm finishing the last chapter of my recipe book and preparing the manuscript to submit to the editor. I'm a lot more confident now as this is my fourth non-fiction book, so I have plenty of experience working with editors and publishers. But with my OCD, the process is taking a bit longer than it should. I want everything perfect. And Myrna, Bobby, and Freddy have been so patient. Along with Solly, everyone makes me feel so appreciated.

The last recipe I'm working on brings me back to the final days of living in Rye Brook, New York, with the children's father, SpaceCowboy Feinman. Let's see if I remember all of the ingredients. Planet- and star-shaped pasta, cubed mozzarella, canola mayo, ranch dressing, diced plum tomatoes, and shredded basil with salt and pepper. Yes, that's it: *Out of This World All-Star Caprese Pasta Salad.* Let me share with you how this recipe came about…

Milagros was totally cool with missing a Sunday for the sake of love. I called her the day after I saw David while SpaceCowboy was at work and the kids were at school and told her the story. She was excited and said, "I miss that feeling. I had it once with my ex-husband. I'm so happy for you." And with that, I had her blessing to get together with my love on Sunday. After all, I'd see her at work on Monday and could go to lunch with her to provide all the dirt.

David was waiting in the parking lot when I got there at around 10:20 a.m. I got out of my car, locked it up, and ran over to him for a familiar bear hug. His mustached smile warmed my heart. We got in his white Olds Cutlass Ciera and drove the hour northwest to his three-bedroom, two-and-a-half-bath townhouse in rural Flower, New York. It looked like a delightful one-horse town with antique shops and a lone True-Value hardware store on Main Street. The town was really only a few blocks long and the elementary, middle, and high schools were all in close proximity.

When we pulled up to his driveway, I saw a large, beautiful home with a two-car garage. It was the spacious center unit of a series of five attached townhouses of which there were over a hundred in this complex. This was a giant leap from David's one-room yellow studio apartment in Lincolndale the last time I saw him in 1980. And it was double the size of SpaceCowboy's co-op in Rye Brook, my home for the last eleven years. I was already impressed because, for some reason, I thought David would still be living small.

He used the remote garage door opener, raised the right door, and pulled in. On the left of the garage, I glanced at floor-to-ceiling wooden storage cabinets he'd had built by a handyman neighbor when Elsie stopped driving in 1990.

She'd had a series of horrific accidents, the first of which occurred in 1987 while they were still living in New Rochelle, when she set herself on fire. Alcohol from her drink spilled on her nightgown and the spark of her cigarette lighter ignited her, burning over sixty percent of her body. Luckily, David was there when it happened, but he had to put the flames out by rolling her on the floor with his bare hands. Although she'd been a smoker for many years, this further damaged her lungs and she spent many days in the hospital burn unit, then subsequently in rehab. Her massive scars prohibited her from working as a flight attendant. David thought it would be beneficial to Elsie's recovery to buy their home in the country. Perhaps a change of scenery…

Elsie went on disability, they bought the home in 1987, and Elsie used her personal savings to hire an interior decorator to redesign the roomy unit. This kept her occupied, but unfortunately did not solve her drinking problem and she had another accident in 1990 when she fell down the stairs, shattering several bones in her legs. David found her at the bottom of the staircase when he came home from work at 6:30 p.m. She had apparently been there almost all day, unable to move.

Two years passed, and by 1992, Elsie was unable to take care of herself. She just quit fighting one afternoon, drank a bottle of rum combined with several bottles of prescription painkillers, and checked out of the pain. David came home again to find her lifeless body sprawled out on the adjustable hospital bed in the master bedroom. She was just a few months short of her fiftieth birthday.

How sorry I felt for Elsie that she had no choice but to end her life. And how sad it was for David who stood by her through all the pain—a loyal and true companion.

So here we were in David's house of memories, looking to make our own memories, and hopefully soon with my two children. We had lots to talk about but David knew that in order to be with me, Lori and Mitchell made it a package deal. His son, Scott, was on his own, in his late twenties, quite successful, and living in New York City.

But remember when David, at forty-five, passed for thirty-five? He was always youthful and confessed to me that he was ready to be a stepfather, especially since he was unable to have children with Elsie due to his vasectomy. At sixty-three, he could have easily passed for fifty. Even though back when I was in my twenties he said he didn't want more children, over the years he'd realized that he missed having a larger family. This would be a dream come true for David as well.

We continued our tour of the downstairs which was tastefully decorated in tones of pink, sage green, and maroon. The rooms were airy and I was happy to see there was a laundry room right off the gigantic kitchen. I would no longer have to *schlep* loads of wash down the elevator to the basement of the co-op building and wait inside the laundry room so nobody would steal my family's clean clothes. I could cook while the washer and dryer did their jobs. Up the pink-carpeted staircase were two bedrooms and a good-sized full bathroom in the hall. The third bedroom, the impressive master, was at the end of the hall and had its own master bath. David and I both agreed we'd need to remove the hospital bed and replace it with a king-size bedroom set. David had been sleeping on the full-size bed in the spare bedroom because he couldn't face the memory of the horror that occurred in the master bedroom. I'd never expected to experience such an elegant domicile having grown up in a tiny, 696-square-foot home in the Bronx.

David and I then went to the spare bedroom to hug and kiss and play and relax a bit before we'd go for some lunch, then head back to pick up my car. It felt like old times and we talked about how I would soon have to break the news to SpaceCowboy.

We had a light lunch at the Goshen Diner where everyone knew David. That apparently became his second home because he went there practically every day for dinner ever since Elsie had passed three years ago. That is, when he wasn't traveling to the casinos in Atlantic City. What the hell? He'd retired immediately after Elsie died—sort of a forced retirement because he hit the magic number of sixty, so IBM offered him a buyout and a decent pension. And David never knew how to cook—he was lucky he could make scrambled eggs, *nebuch* (such a pity; poor thing).

As we entered the mirrored, old-school diner right off the Goshen exit on Route 17, David introduced me to all the waitresses he knew by their first names. After his grilled cheese and tomato and my tuna salad platter, we were back on the Quickway, heading to my car at the Holidome. The following week would be Thanksgiving, so we knew we wouldn't see each other for a while. I told him I'd call him on my lunch breaks from work and he said he'd try to have my cell phone ready by the next time we'd get together. Back in 1995, it took a while to order and make arrangements with the phone company. We agreed that

I'd talk with SpaceCowboy before the Goldman Thanksgiving get-together next Thursday.

Back in Rye Brook, I had a few minutes to ponder this monumental transition before SpaceCowboy would arrive home with Lori and Mitchell from Queens. Monday night wouldn't be a good time to speak with him because Mitchell had his tae kwon do lesson after school while Lori had her dance lesson. Afterwards, we'd shuffle with homework, dinner, baths, then stories. That left Tuesday and hopefully once, and *if,* he and I could reach some sort of agreement, we'd figure out a way to speak to the kids on Wednesday, the day before the big family Thanksgiving gathering—maybe even look for a good children's therapist to work with us. I was sure this would be wise.

My brain was spinning when I realized I had a mind-bending headache. Within the next few months, I would lose forty pounds from the destruction of one family and the rebuilding of another.

At around 7:30 p.m., as the Tylenol was numbing the pounding in my skull, I heard the key in the lock, then little feet scrambling through the living room. "Mommy, look what Pop-Pop and *Bubbe* gave us," Mitchell squealed with delight and showed me a little cardboard airplane which he and Pop-Pop painted blue and red. And Lori loved her gift, a big purple plush teddy bear she named Patsy, after the kids' favorite country singer, Patsy Cline. These kids just made me smile.

After the kids went to sleep, I thought, *what the hell am I doing?* Do I stay in a loveless marriage after thirteen years like Mommy and Daddy had for forty-one? Or do I make a grab for the golden ring and take a gigantic leap for love? I'd probably need more than Tylenol, but I'd taken a hiatus from weed when precocious Lori was about three and she found a roach in the master bathroom.

She knew her dad was in a stop-smoking (cigarettes) program (complete with electric shock therapy—could that account for the strange behavior?), so she thought that the quarter-joint was a cigarette butt and said to me, "Daddy's at it again." After that embarrassment, I vowed to never have pot in the house or anywhere near the children.

Tuesday, I called SpaceCowboy at work and asked him if we could schedule a little talk after the kids went to bed. He said, "Absolutely, I've wanted to talk to you, too," which was odd because he didn't talk much to anyone but the kids and to his space digests. So after Lori and Mitchell were in dreamland, their dad and I sat down in the living room.

"Joe, I'm not sure this environment is good for Lori and Mitchell. We rarely talk…" I began.

"Well, I think you're right and there's something you need to know," Joe interrupted calmly.

He continued, "I wasn't being entirely honest with you when I told you about my business trip a few weeks ago. I did go to Tampa, but not to RUB's offices. I applied for a job at Einstein Space Center. The field is geriatric studies in space travel. You see, I'm finally getting my wish." I didn't know if I should faint or do the happy dance. I let him continue.

"I'd been corresponding with HR there and sent them my résumé a few months ago. The trip and interview were just formalities because it's still a relatively new field and there weren't a lot of applicants. They say I have a strong background and my health is good." I just let it sink in while I took a deep breath and for once in my life thought before I spoke. The pressure on me was off because now I could do whatever I wanted. And right now, I wanted to move to Flower, New York.

Take a deep breath, Fanny. "Wow, I'm happy for you," I told the truth. I didn't even have to mention David and chose not to, at least for a while, so we could get the wheels rolling. I figured Joe would have to sell his co-op and the kids and I would have to live *somewhere*, so *my* details could wait until *his* were set in stone. And if that *somewhere* just happened to be Flower, New York—oh well. By then, hopefully, he'd be too far along with his cosmological preparations to back out.

Wednesday morning, I was actually able to make a same-day after-school appointment with a well-known local family therapist who came highly recommended through my friend Enid—you remember, the gal with the four children by two different husbands—and I called SpaceCowboy at work. I asked if he could possibly leave work early enough to meet me at four p.m. at Dr. Melinda Samberg's office in Greenwich, Connecticut, and found out that Enid had canceled her son's appointment so we could get in. I really did owe Enid a lot and when I called later on to thank her, she just said, "Come on, wouldn't you do that for me?"

SpaceCowboy called me back a few minutes later to say, "Of course, you're paying for the co-pay for the shrink visit, right?" Cheapskate. But I didn't care. I was free—almost.

I picked Lori and Mitchell up at school and because I said we had to go to the doctor, they thought they were going to their pediatrician. I explained it was a doctor our family would just go and talk to and they seemed intrigued. SpaceCowboy walked in at 3:50 p.m. and the kids ran over to hug their daddy. Dr. Samberg, who strongly resembled Barbra Streisand as Fanny Brice in *Funny Girl*, took us promptly at four and SpaceCowboy and I agreed to slowly reveal the plan for our separation. SpaceCowboy and I had had a conference call with Dr. Samberg earlier in the day to fill her in on what was going on so she would guide us on the best way to cushion the blow for the children.

"Mommy and Daddy wanted to speak with both of you about some things that will be changing pretty soon with our lives," began SpaceCowboy. "You know how much Daddy loves learning about the stars and planets and space travel?" Both kids nodded.

He always spoke in third person. "Well, Daddy has to take a new job, but it won't be here in New York. Daddy will be moving to Tampa, Florida, so I can work at the Einstein Space Center. I may even be traveling in outer space soon!"

The kids seemed puzzled, and first Lori said, "But I don't want to live in Tampa—I want to stay here in New York!"

And Mitchell followed with, "No, I'm staying where Lori and Mommy are." They were quite clear with their desires, it seemed.

So Dr. Samberg asked us how we planned to work this all out. I suggested that Lori and Mitchell would visit with their daddy on holidays, long weekends, and whenever SpaceCowboy could arrange a vacation from this new job. Lori, and especially Mitchell, seemed thrilled with the idea of taking an airplane to visit their daddy, as Mitchell was still full throttle with his desire to become a commercial pilot when he grew up.

Then Mitchell and Lori realized that we wouldn't be living together as a family and both started to cry. But SpaceCowboy and I promptly assured them, with hugs and kisses, that we both would love them forever—that would never change—and that they might eventually go to live somewhere else with Mommy after Daddy sold the co-op.

SpaceCowboy had about a month before he would start his job at Einstein Space Center—just after the New Year, 1996, so he agreed to allow us to stay in his co-op until the summer. He would list it to sell in the spring. The real estate for that particular building was booming; units usually sold after only a few weeks—a month tops. So the kids would be able to finish out the year in their current school and move over the summer—wherever I decided—to start the new school year in September 1996 in a different school.

Dr. Samberg wished us well, assuring us that we could see her again if the kids or we had any issues to discuss with her. We thanked her.

We all met for the last time as the Goldman-Feinman family for Thanksgiving at Harry's and Karen's in Yonkers. Along with the cranberry-orange-walnut relish, I brought my *Out of This World All-Star Caprese Pasta Salad* to commemorate and celebrate, in my own way, SpaceCowboy's forthcoming new life. I made it with planet- and star-shaped pasta, cubed mozzarella, canola mayo, ranch dressing, diced plum tomatoes and shredded basil with salt and pepper. In addition to the turkey and stuffing, everyone agreed it was the standout best side dish.

When all the nieces and nephews were playing in one of the bedrooms after dinner, SpaceCowboy and I announced that we'd be parting ways, and filled in all the adults with details, including my older brother Marty and his wife Wanda. No one was shocked because they knew SpaceCowboy was weird and had this *Rainman* thing for space travel. Marty said, "So that's why you made the space pasta salad."

Then, Harry pulled me in the kitchen before we left and asked, "So, what happened with David?" And of course, I told him everything. He wondered why I didn't fight for half of the co-op, but I said I was about to get a large, three-bedroom, two-and-a-half-bath home in lovely Flower, New York, so I didn't need the aggravation. And SpaceCowboy was shrewd legally, so I didn't have the energy or inclination to fight with him now that I would be back with my one true love. I also told Harry that I was waiting patiently and, I felt, wisely to make *any* move until SpaceCowboy was firmly planted in Tampa, and maybe even in outer space.

twenty

David Tobin, Redux

Well, I finally did it. My new cookbook, *Fanny on Fire*, is in the hands of my young editor, Bruce Goose. Yes, folks, that's his real name. Myrna and Bobby had Mandiyee pitch my book to the same literary agent that sold Canadian chef Cody Banks' book, *Eating from Shore to Shore*. So my agent, Ina Schnurer—I call her "I'm a *schnoorer* (I'm a moocher, a sponger, a taker)" behind her back—sent my book proposal out to Masterpiece Food Publishers on the Lower East Side and they grabbed it. I only wish it had been *that* easy with my first three books I wrote about inventions and Chinese manufacturing years ago.

It's great to have connections, but I'm spending every waking moment yelling and screaming at the changes Bruce Goose wants to make with my recipes and chapter intros. These are recipes that I created, tested, and tasted, so why do I have to change them? He's not even freakin' Jewish, so what the hell does he know about Jewish-style cooking? *Oy*. Let me see if I can talk to Myrna and Bobby. But right now, we're about to go into a segment...

"Ladies and gents, it's my pleasure to introduce you to today's guest, Cody Banks, accomplished chef and star of FUC's hit show, *From Canada with Love*," I said as I waved Cody over to my counter to shake his hand. Cody is tall and cute with blonde, shaggy hair and about forty. He had a large photo button of his new baby daughter, Ottawa Banks, pinned on to the top seam of his apron.

I said, "What a *zeeskeit* (sweetie, cutie-pie), but why the unusual name?"

Cody said, "Well, she was conceived when my wife and I were on vacation in our nation's capital." *Oy*, these young folks. What's wrong with a normal name like *Yankel, Latifah,* or *Chaneleh*?

"The main ingredient of today's delicious recipe is one that a lot of Jewish folks have been using for many generations. Jews love smoked salmon and salmon croquettes. And Cody was kind enough to bring some fresh Pacific salmon with him today, so let's get cracking," I said as I placed the filet on the cutting board.

"How'd you all like to learn how to make a salmon bake with orange-zested butter and peas?" I asked our imaginary audience. "Cody, here, you get the aluminum foil ready."

"So, Fanny, I'm *aboot* to put some vegetable spray on the foil so the salmon doesn't stick, *eh*?" said Cody. "With this dish, it's all *aboot* the orange zest and melted butter, *eh*?"

At first, I thought my ears were playing tricks but Cody continued, "We add salt, pepper, onion powder, and garlic powder to the fillet. Then we add *aboot* a cup and a half of peas over the fish before we drizzle on the orange zest, orange juice, and melted butter, *eh*?"

By now, I'd had it with this guy's accent and asked him, "What *boot* are you talking about? I don't wear boots; I wear flip-flops. And are you freakin' hard of hearing? You keep on asking, '*eh*? What the hell is that?"

With that, Cody said with a smile, "That's just how we speak in Canada, *eh* folks? I was kind of thinking you had a thick Bronx accent, but at least I used self-restraint." Touché. One of these days I'll learn to filter, but I was really glad Cody had a good sense of humor.

We finished the salmon foil packet and it was destined for a 400-degree oven for *aboot* thirty minutes. After a commercial break, out came the hot, orange-scented delight which Cody proceeded to plate while adding a drizzle of the orange-butter sauce atop the peas and salmon on our classic lavender plates. We each grabbed a fork and I closed with "Friends, thanks to today's guest, Cody Banks, star of *From Canada with Love*. Today it was all *aboot* the salmon!"

While SpaceCowboy prepared for his move to Tampa, I made it a point to speak to David almost every day using the newfangled cell phone he bought me. I kept it hidden and turned off in my tote bag because it was a huge monstrosity of a thing that must have weighed at least two or three pounds. I used to charge it at work or on my days off when SpaceCowboy wasn't home because I still didn't want to arouse any suspicions. I was hoping I could pull off everything we'd been planning. David was as patient as ever and I...not so much. But I figured we'd waited over fifteen years to finally be together again, so this ain't so bad.

We did have to schedule some sessions with Dr. Samberg because Lori was having nightmares and Mitchell began to use profanities in school. Dr. Samberg was helpful to both children using play therapy. Lori chose dolls and Mitchell drew pictures of airplanes. And they had joint sessions using Beanie Babies as Mommy, Daddy, Lori, and Mitchell. SpaceCowboy took them for a few sessions when he could, and after a while, both children seemed to understand that they would always see their daddy and that he'd be just a phone call and a plane ride away. It's just our living arrangements that would be changing.

I continued to see David on Sundays when SpaceCowboy took the children to Queens or on days when I was off from work thanks to my part-time schedule. We talked about plans for the big move, hopefully sometime in the summer. SpaceCowboy finally made *his* move during the week between Christmas and New Year's Eve by renting a U-Haul and rounding up some workers from the local Rye Brook migrant worker pick-up zone. What, did you think he'd use a professional mover even though Einstein Space Center was paying his relocation expenses?

The apartment looked a little empty, but that was only because he took with him all the space digests that were scattered throughout the house. He had few other possessions as he wore the same three or four button-down shirts all the time—the ones I thought he looked cute in fourteen years ago. He did remember to take the old car salvage parts he'd gotten over the years from the junk yard that were stored top-to-bottom in the co-op building's basement storage bin.

Lori and Mitchell hugged him tightly and he promised to see them on the next school vacation. I was fine with that because even though SpaceCowboy and I had little in common, we shared a love for those two precious *kinderlach* (children). We'd let the lawyers work everything else out.

Spring vacation, early April 1996: The kids were excited to be taking a plane down to Tampa to visit their daddy. Mitchell, although he was only seven, knew in advance which airline to choose, what model plane they'd be flying in, and told us the most reasonable flight times to select. This little boy's already a *mensch*, I thought.

Lori had a cute purple Teen Queen carry-on packed with granola bars, little goldfish crackers, *reenies*, and juice boxes, which she would share with her brother. Mitchell had a Superman royal blue carry-on which he had packed with—what else?—his little toy planes of every shape and size and some crayons and coloring books for the long flight. The airline knew in advance that the kids would be flying unescorted, but back then, pre-9/11 and pre-TSA, parents were permitted to bring their children up to the gates and wait with them until the plane was loaded. And their fairly reliable daddy, SpaceCowboy, would be waiting for them at the gate when they arrived in Tampa. Lori, at almost twelve, was quite mature, very skilled at looking after her brother, and had taken a Red Cross babysitting course the year before.

"Call me from a pay phone at the airport in Tampa when you land," I begged them after a group hug. Lori had a pocketful of change for the phone.

"We will, Mommy!" said both as they boarded.

Next thing I remembered, later that evening, just after David arrived to spend a few days with me at the co-op in Rye Brook—and I'd hoped that we wouldn't run into any of the neighbors—the phone rang and I picked it up to hear both Lori's and Mitchell's excited voices.

"Mommy, I got another set of wings from the pilot! And Daddy has a girlfriend named Rona!" said Mitchell. Then I heard Lori shush Mitchell in the background but he persisted. "And we all went to White Castle for dinner. Daddy had five hamburgers, Lori had two cheeseburgers, I had a sack of chicken rings, and Rona had French fries because she said she's a *vegamarian*."

Oy, so he hooked up with a *tchatchke* (little toy or knick-knack, slang for girlfriend), and he was down there not even three months. And a vegetarian to boot! I was laughing to myself because all this was simply perfect. The pressure really *was* off; I would no longer have to hide David from my life or from the kids. Thank you, Rona Ditzman. SpaceCowboy was not one to remain woman-less for any long periods of time, anyway. After all, he and I met less than a month after he was divorced from wifey-poo number one, another red flag I conveniently chose to ignore so many years ago.

It turned out Rona Ditzman was also an accomplished research scientist who hailed from Brooklyn by way of Riverdale, New York. She was also recently transplanted to Tampa for the geriatric studies in space travel program, along with her ten-year-old daughter, Louise. Lori and Mitchell were excited that they'd be meeting Louise on their next trip to Tampa over the summer because Louise was visiting her dad in Riverdale during this Easter-Passover break.

David and I were busy playing doctor in the king-size bed when I noticed a lack of tobacco scent on him that was normally difficult to conceal due to my severe allergies. I began to sniff around when David pulled out a can of Charms assorted fruit candies from his canvas overnight bag, offered me some, and then grabbed a green one for himself.

"See, I told you I could stop smoking," he smiled proudly. I was thrilled because now that he was getting older, I'd want to spend as much time as I could with this man. Within less than a dozen years, I would find out just how dangerous his previous smoking habit would prove, but right now I had my smoke-free honey in my bed.

SpaceCowboy listed the co-op for sale with a local realtor, Rye Brook Properties, at the end of April. He agreed to arrange viewings only when I was at work, the kids were at school, or when we'd have enough time to be elsewhere so as not to further traumatize Lori and Mitchell. At the same time, I told SpaceCowboy that I had reunited with David Tobin and he had a magnificent three-bedroom townhome in rural, upstate Flower, New York. SpaceCowboy knew the area because he'd worked the Catskills hotel circuit during the summers while he was a college student. And because he now had Rona, all he could say was, "Well, it sounds like a nice place to live." And surely it soon would be.

During Memorial Day weekend, I pulled the kids out from school a day early on Friday. I arranged for them to come with me to check out life in Flower, New York. On the long ride up, I told Lori and Mitchell that they were going to meet an old friend of mine whom I knew before I met their daddy and that he was a kind and funny man. I also told them they'd be seeing a new neighborhood and getting their own private tour of two new schools. They seemed curious and asked many questions, but, having adjusted well to their daddy's living in another part of the country, they began to take new experiences in stride thanks to Dr. Samberg and parents who loved them.

Lori thought the schools were smaller, less crowded, and more "cozy," as she put it, than the larger Rye Brook schools and she thought the village was pretty. However, she and Mitchell seemed concerned with making new friends.

"What if the girls don't like me and what if they don't like my clothes?" asked Lori with quite legitimate pre-teen concerns.

But, just as we were driving up to David's driveway and they were climbing out of my car, the school bus was dropping off kids from the development at around 3:15 p.m. Both Lori and Mitchell glanced, wide-eyed, as three children ran off the bus at the stop by the mail drop. There were two boys who were heading to the house next door, one older and one younger than Mitchell, while a girl who looked about Lori's age headed to a house three doors away. Was this divine intervention?

Mitchell pulled out a toy airplane and ran over to show it to the boys, whom he later found out were brothers named Gary and Tommy. And Vanessa, rather than running home into an empty house, watched as the three boys planted themselves in the driveway to talk about toys. Lori introduced herself and said she lived in Rye Brook, New York, but just had a tour of the school in Flower. We later found out that Vanessa was a latchkey child whose mom worked at the nearby hospital, so she was alone for about two hours each day after school.

I made no attempt to call the kids into the house to meet David because this was a good sign; they weren't in the village for more than a few hours and they had made friends. Eventually, I called David on the cell phone and he opened up the garage door to a bunch of smiling kids. I casually introduced Lori and Mitchell to David and they ran to shake hands with a quick, "Hi." I always insisted on good manners.

David grinned and whispered to me, "Fanny, Lori looks just like you. And Mitchell reminds me of Scott and all the energy he had when he was that age. Ya' did good, Muffy!" I hugged him and said that I remembered Scott when he was just about Mitchell's age now. Muffy was an endearing moniker David had given me when we lived together so many years ago, but I had no idea where it came from. I never did get to ask him its origin, but knowing David, it probably referred to a nickname for the female anatomy.

When Gary, Tommy, and Vanessa all went in for dinner, we took Lori and Mitchell inside for a tour of David's home. We had bought a blue metal bunk bed for what would be Mitchell's room and decorated both top and bottom bunks with Teenage Mutant Ninja Turtles comforters in case he wanted to have a sleepover. And we dressed up what would be Lori's room with the comfy old full-size bed that David had used before we got rid of the hospital bed along with the bad memories in the master bedroom. Lori would come to love her pastel-colored comforter with matching pillows and window curtains. She had a huge walk-in closet she could load with pre-teen clothes we were sure she'd be buying at the nearby Galleria shopping mall. Maybe she'd go shopping with her new friend Vanessa. Even David and I had a spanking new king-size oak bed wall set in the master suite.

Everyone agreed on peanut butter and jelly sandwiches for dinner that night which was lucky because that was about all David had in the house. We'd have to do some serious food shopping soon and luckily there was a second fridge in the garage that would eventually be home to my many frozen Tupperware portions of leftover homemade delicacies.

Back in Rye Brook, I made every effort to make the co-op sellable, including heating up homemade potpourri on the stove in a pot filled with water, vanilla, and cinnamon sticks whenever potential buyers were coming for a look. The whole apartment smelled sweet. As we suspected, the unit sold within a few weeks and SpaceCowboy arranged to come back in July for the closing. He would also take Lori and Mitchell back to Tampa with him for a few weeks as he'd been working at Einstein for six months by then and managed to get some vacation time. This would give me time to pack with David and then hire a moving company to help with the relocation.

David's mom, Patty, and her third husband, Benny, were in visiting from Boynton Beach, Florida, staying at David's half-sister's house in Pelham, New York. I had first met Patty, a petite old Jewish woman, in 1978 when David and I were on vacation in Fort Lauderdale, Florida. She was married to her second husband back then. It turns out that she was quite the number in her mid-sixties, as she had all the men coming to call the day after hubby number two kicked the bucket back in 1979. Hubby number one was David's dad, Moses, and they had divorced when David was a pre-schooler in the mid-1930s.

I decided to invite Patty, who was now in her early eighties; Benny, a few years younger; and Renée, David's half-sister; and her husband, Mike, to dinner at David's right before I moved in. I had also met Renée and Mike when I was with David the first time around when they were young-marrieds living in Staten Island in the late seventies. We used to take Scott there on David's weekend visitation days, usually Sundays. While Renée was never warm back then, I thought, hey, it's fifteen years later. Maybe after she had a daughter of her own she'd be nicer? No greater Jewish-American princess stereotype ever existed. For some reason she seemed jealous of me, perhaps thinking I was vying for her mother's attention and inheritance? No thank you. She even once told David, "Mommy always liked you best." Poor, delusional Renée.

David had driven down to Pelham earlier to pick up Patty and Benny so they could come and stay with us for a few days while Lori and Mitchell were visiting with their dad in Tampa. Then, Renée and Mike would come for dinner and take her mom and step-dad back with them to Pelham. Patty and I prepared ten good-sized salmon fillets—about five pounds' worth—and arranged them on two cookie sheets. Renée and Mike were due for dinner at six, so at around 5:30 p.m., I put the salmon in the oven, figuring the large pieces might take a little longer than usual to cook.

Well, six came and went, as did seven, and by around eight p.m., while the filets were set on the "stay warm" setting in the oven, Patty wisely said, "Okay— you could probably keep them moist by dabbing a little mayo on top. Then cover them in foil." And dinner was barely salvageable just as Renée and Mike finally rang the doorbell at 8:15 p.m. to say, "Sorry, we were stuck in traffic." They had cell phones, so they could have called us. That would not be the only time Renée showed her true colors. And the overdone salmon made me look like a shitty cook.

Meanwhile, Milagros and I spoke often, so she knew I'd soon be moving away from Rye Brook. As controller and HR chief at our job, she also counseled me, wisely, to give at least two weeks' notice to the owners of Land-Ocean Imports. During my brief conference with Lauren and Malcolm Silverman, because I'd been there already several years and felt comfortable with this older couple, I told them about my moving in with David. I explained I had known him many years before. I said I'd be divorcing the children's father and spoke a bit about SpaceCowboy's story of finding his true passion for space travel.

I was amused when Lauren said, "Wow, you should write a memoir someday," and pleasantly surprised when she asked if I'd like to stay on as a consultant—perhaps for one or two days per week—while Lori and Mitchell were in school.

Because I really didn't want to leave this job I'd come to love, I immediately jumped off my chair and ran over to hug the kind couple. "Thanks ever so much!"

I was certain that Milagros had something to do with this offer. I was also sure it would be fine with David, who was retired and would be happy to stay with Lori and Mitchell for a few hours after school if I happened to get stuck in traffic on the long ride home. And that is how FannyGo Consulting came about and how my salary automatically doubled to a high hourly consultant's rate.

A few days later, before the kids returned from Tampa, David and I orchestrated the move from Rye Brook to Flower, New York. Both Lori and Mitchell knew they'd be returning to their new home, so it was not a surprise. They also knew they'd be permitted to take whatever they wanted to David's house because it was double the size of their old apartment. Having room for everything would not be an issue.

David suggested he and I go to the mall and get two new toys for the kids as a welcome gift. He chose a little brown, funny-faced, stuffed monkey for Mitchell and a red-headed Cabbage Patch doll for Lori. When they returned, in addition to gossiping about meeting Louise, Rona's daughter, in Tampa— "Mommy," said the like-mother-like-son, unfiltered Mitchell. "She has buck teeth like Rona!"—both were thrilled with their new toys which they promptly named "Beeter" and "Lynn Leah."

twenty-one
Life in the Country

"Hi Tina, this is Fanny Goldman," I said as I spoke into my office phone. I was nervous because I wasn't sure if Freddy's unusual behavior over the past few months was something that was manifesting only at work, or if Tina had noticed anything different.

"Oh, hi Fanny! How've you been?" whispered Tina at the other end, sounding exhausted. "Freddy's in the bathroom, but I've wanted to speak with you. Myrna and Bobby said that Freddy's been doing weird things at the studio."

"*Oy*, Tina," I said as I proceeded to tell her about his mini mental lapses back to 1978 and his verbal indiscretions with our show's guests. Tina, Freddy's wife of over thirty years, was not in any way shocked.

"I was afraid of that. I've been watching him carefully. At first, I thought it was the pot, but he's been smoking that for a long, long time," said Tina calmly. "I've made an appointment with our primary care doc here in Pleasantville for next week. I told Freddy we were both due for physicals and he was okay with that." Wow, if this were my hubby, I'd be a wreck.

I promised Tina we'd all keep an eye on Freddy for her over the next few weeks and let her know if anything else unusual came up. "Be well, Tina *dahlink*, and let me know if there's anything else I can do to help," I said in a forced cheery

163

voice because I didn't want her to know how concerned I'd been for her husband.

The next day, I got a surprise delivery at my dressing room door. The Famous Pleasantville Bakery's amazing *rugelach* (a sweet, Jewish mini-pastry)—a four-pound box of assorted delights. Apricot, raspberry, chocolate, and cinnamon with a card signed, "Thanks, Tina." What a gem—a class act. I'd have to put them out in the reception area because these are so good I could eat all four pounds myself. Then Fanny's fashions would no longer fit her fanny.

Settling into a blissful life in the country was not a hardship. I finally had my man whom I'd loved for almost half my life. My dreams really did come true. He was simply as good to me as he had been back in the seventies. He took care of the bills courtesy of his generous IBM pension and social security. David was kind and funny with Lori and Mitchell as they adapted rather well into the Flower, New York, school system and their various extra-curricular activities. Mitchell continued with his tae kwon do classes, this time at our development's clubhouse, and Lori played the mellophone in the marching band and the French horn in the school orchestra.

Once or twice a week, I'd drive down to Rye Brook as soon as the kids left for school and consult at Land-Sea Imports for a few hours clearing up messes by auditing invoices issued by the customs brokers for recent shipments imported from China. Malcolm and Lauren knew that with my OCD tendencies, I'd never miss a billing error for import duties. Over the years, I'd saved them thousands of dollars by spotting adjustments their brokers would subsequently need to report to US Customs.

Eventually, by 2001, with over twenty-five years of international trade experience at the time, I would have my own customs broker license, having passed the rigorous exam held at the government building on Varick Street in New York City less than a month after 9/11.

When I knew in advance which days I'd be working, I always made sure to bring in a dish I could share with my office mates. I was beginning to gain a reputation for tasty Jewish specialties. And I looked forward to catching up with Milagros. Even though I was working part-time, I'd take a half-hour lunch to sit and chat with her in the break room. Occasionally, on weekends, Lori, Mitchell, and I would drive down to Westchester to visit their favorite *tía* (aunt), Milagros.

The divorce process took almost two and a half years. Part of it was because of the difficulty in scheduling court appearances due to SpaceCowboy's distance. Mostly, though, it was because attorneys who practice family and matrimonial law rank highest on my list of low-life pond scum. The more delays they can arrange, the more paperwork they can create. Even though it was a fairly simple, uncontested matter, add a law guardian for the children to the mix and we were basically paying for their summer homes and possibly the college education of the children of not two, but three motherfucking juris doctors. I only wish I knew then what I know now; I would have suggested mediation.

About $150,000 later, we had a fairly good indication that the divorce would be final by early *Pesach* 1998. Looking back, I should have listened to Missy, the prudent bookkeeper at Chemical Commodities, when she said to take it easy and not rush into marriage with Joe/SpaceCowboy so many years ago. Missy said, "Don't get married unless you are one hundred percent certain you are in love." And now I was sure I had repeated my parents' unhappy marriage when I'd married Joe/SpaceCowboy. How glad I was to be able to break this pattern and marry again, this time for love.

David's mom and step-dad were visiting again from Boynton Beach, so in a matter of just a few days we had to pull off locating a rabbi and scheduling a temple on what would turn out to be exactly one week after my divorce decree was stamped "4/3/98." Of course, we wanted David's parents present. I called around Orange County, New York, on the recommendations of a few locals, but the trick was that Friday, April 10, 1998, would be the first Seder night of Passover and only one Reform rabbi was willing to do a wedding right before the holiday. A conservative or an Orthodox rabbi wouldn't have been an option because I didn't have a *get* (religious, complicated Jewish divorce). There was no fucking way Fanny was gonna get a *get*.

We spoke on the phone with Rabbi Joffee at the New Windsor Jewish Community Center and he agreed to perform our wedding ceremony at 11:30 a.m. He had to be out by early afternoon to help his wife prepare for his family's Passover meal. He told us what to bring and said he'd have a *chuppah* (ritual canopy for Jewish weddings), which was reassuring because we had just the one week to pull off getting a marriage license, ordering flowers, and finding a dress for me and a dress for Lori who would be my junior maid of honor.

April 10, 1998: David and I asked a local couple with whom we were fairly friendly, Jon and Sandy, to serve as witnesses and to sign our *Ketubah* (Hebrew marriage license). I already knew that my best friends Cami and Milagros would be unable to attend the ceremony because it coincided with Good Friday and both gals were devout Catholics. My brothers also didn't make it because Marty's wife was Episcopalian and Harry's wife was Catholic, so we did manage to schedule a wham-bang reception for Sunday, April 19. Obviously, my mom, Jane Goldman, couldn't make it either because by then she was almost eighty and Harry, who still lived in Yonkers—close to our old Bronx family domicile—was her sole source of transportation. By April 19, Passover and Easter would have come and gone, so everyone would be free to celebrate our big day, even if it was nine days after the fact.

David looked distinguished and handsome in his navy blue pinstripe suit, white shirt, and red tie. He wore a white *kippah*. I wore a gently-flowing, soft printed, sage green flowered midi dress with a white lace collar and white pumps. I had a white and sage green bouquet and a white flower clip in my hair. Lori also had a flower print dress, but hers was pastel-colored and she wore white pumps as well, with a pastel-colored flower hair clip. Mitchell had a navy blue vest and slacks, a light blue shirt, and navy tie. Lori, at thirteen and a half, was a mini-me. And Mitchell, at nine and a half, was still as cute as a button.

Eleven-thirty came and went and I should have known what to expect.

By 1:30 p.m., Rabbi Joffee said that he'd have to leave within another half hour, by two. We kept on apologizing and Lori even went to try, unsuccessfully, to reach Renée at her home number because we didn't have her cell info.

Finally, at 1:45 p.m., the errant, irresponsible *mishpocheh* (family) entered the sanctuary. Renée led the tribe, prancing in her black stilettos and inappropriately-tight leopard-print mini dress, towering over her husband, Mike the Weasel, who trailed behind her. Also in the entourage were their teenage daughter, Jennifer, David's son, Scott, and Patty and Benny, who both looked embarrassed.

"So sorry; we had to make sure the caterers had everything just right for the Seder tonight," was Renée's fucked up excuse for being late for her half-brother's wedding.

In a brief, but touching fifteen-minute ceremony, with our friends Jon and Sandy holding two of the four *chuppah* poles, Renée chewing gum at the third pole, and Scott at the fourth pole, Rabbi Joffee pronounced us husband and wife. David stomped on the glass with gleeful "*Mazel tovs*" from Patty and Benny, and even from Lori and Mitchell. My sweetheart kissed his new Mrs. David Tobin, the rabbi signed the *ketubah*, wished us well, and almost tripped on the runner in the aisle as he ran to the parking lot at exactly two p.m.

Now, of course, we were way late for the one p.m. lunch reservations we'd had at Fortuna's Italian Restaurant just about a mile north of the temple. Luckily, because there were twelve of us, with a quick, apologetic call before we left the temple, they were all too happy to receive us, albeit an hour and a half late.

After a tasty Northern Italian feast, Renée and posse headed to their undoubtedly perfectly-executed Seder in Pelham, Sandy and Jon back to Flower, New York, while the newlyweds, Mr. and Mrs. David Tobin, drove Lori and Mitchell down to Riverdale. There, they would connect with SpaceCowboy and Rona for a few days during spring break. This way, we could have a proper wedding night. It seemed odd that Rona and Louise always held Seders with her Portuguese Catholic ex-husband Leon just because he loved potato *kugel* (pudding), a common Passover staple.

We drove directly from Riverdale in the North Bronx to the Ramada in Elmsford where we celebrated our wedding night after a dinner of Chinese fusion food at a new restaurant up Route 9A between Elmsford and Hawthorne. After a little TV in the hotel room, both of us fell fast asleep like an old married couple. It was a long day and besides, we'd been sleeping together for a long time by then. My insomnia was still fairly under control in 1998 prior to the worst profanity I've ever uttered: The Big M—Menopause. With the "Do Not Disturb" sign on the doorknob, we both awoke at around nine a.m. and consummated our marriage that following morning.

Though I'd had Renée's number for a long time, David and I agreed to go to the second Seder night at her house, but only because his parents were still in town. Renée was beginning to piss David off as well once he, too, realized her many negative, dislikable personality traits. Her Seders—and all holiday meals for that matter—were orchestrated like a Broadway play. And she was an award-winning actress. "You *must* follow the place cards." "No, you don't have to help clear the table for the next course; that's why I have a maid, darling."

The worst experience, by far, happened at this second Seder night, which was David's and my first official day of wedded bliss. Now, you know that I'm allergic to dogs, so it was already a monumental effort for me to consent to go to Renée's. But I loved David's mother and she loved having her family together whenever they were in town. I took a non-drowsy antihistamine, which didn't always work, before we got there.

We were all seated, having the main course which was a pot roast with a rich sauce made by, of course, the caterers and not Renée. Goddess forbid she should break a fingernail. Beverly, their mangy beagle, jumped up to the center of the big table and knocked down the ritual Seder plate and the satin-covered matzo plate. She then went around the table, stopping at everyone's plates to sniff, slobber, and then eat all the pot roast off each dish.

I gasped and looked at David who was equally as shocked, when Renée's husband, Mike the Weasel, blurted out, "Our poor dog, Beverly, can't even eat at the Seder table with her family. Beverly loves to play this game at mealtime. Just because Fanny's allergic."

He added, "We certainly don't want Beverly to get hurt, so we always keep our wine glasses in the kitchen." Fucking drunk. I'm not entirely sure the health department would approve of this act. We left hungry, too.

From then on, David and I, and Lori and Mitchell when they were available, traveled down to Boynton Beach, Florida, to be with Patty and Benny whenever we could. We avoided Renée and Mike the Weasel like the *Hasidim* avoid bacon.

Then there was our intimate, lovely wedding reception brunch, on Sunday, April 19, 1998, for fifty close friends and family members. While all of the invitations read one p.m., we told Renée and Mike the Weasel, who were, of course, escorting David's mom and step-dad, that it started at twelve noon. Surprise! They actually arrived at one p.m. so we were grateful that David had the foresight to think of this shrewd plan. We knew by now that they'd be at least an hour late for appointments.

David's son, Scott, now a grown businessman at twenty-eight, toasted us, telling the story of how we met in 1977. He added that had we gotten married back then, we might have avoided all the *mishugoss* (craziness, insanity) that occurred during the past twenty years. But, he added that he wouldn't have a stepbrother and stepsister, and for this he was grateful. We all raised our glasses and shouted "*L'chaim!*"

The DJ, Thunder Rollz, played our wedding song, a beautiful oldie whose chorus began with "Tell me you'll love me for a million years…" After we finished our dance, several of the husky male guests grabbed two chairs and hoisted both David and me into the air while the DJ played "Hava Nagila."Brunch was served buffet style and we had a little of everything: chicken, fish, meatballs, and sausages (no, it was not kosher) with a variety of potatoes and veggies. A big salad bowl with croutons was a hit with everyone, even the vegetarians. The DJ played all the right songs, which catered to young and old. We then cut the enormous wedding cake which was, of course, chocolate inside with a lavender frosting.

SpaceCowboy Feinman married Rona Ditzman exactly one month later in Riverdale, New York. Rona's ex-husband, Leon, had acquired a justice of the peace license and married the two of them with Lori, Mitchell, and Louise present. It was a match made in heaven, and the stars, and the planets, and the galaxy. They were both, literally, space cadets.

twenty-two

Monkey Business and Sad Chicken Soup

I was so nervous I wanted to bite my nails, but I didn't want to ruin my purple gel manicure. We were starting my book tour at the Bull by the Horns Casino in upstate Verona, New York. I had to look it up because I had no idea where the hell it was—somewhere just about midpoint between Utica and Syracuse along I-90 in the freakin' boonies. But, at least it was a start.

Bobby said, "Get ready for all the press."

I said, "Thanks; I'm ready. Reminds me of when I first started out with FannyGo Consulting." It also reminded me of writing for both a local newspaper and magazine and then my first book. Then there were book signings, radio interviews, and more…

FUC invited Prairie Tree, famous Native American chef and prolific cookbook author, to accompany me on this joint book launch party. Shiny, long, black braids, tan skin, and high cheek bones were a sharp contrast to her unexpected baby blue eyes. Who knows, maybe she was a direct descendant of Pocahontas and John Rolfe of England, unless she was just wearing blue contacts. Her newest book, *First American Meals,* was a big hit, though Myrna said, "*Fanny on Fire* is already on the track to blockbuster status."

Prairie Tree and I had one of the stages in the vast, futuristic casino.

171

Mandiyee, with her blonde hair back in a bun for sanitary purposes—neither Duni-B nor Puff could make it—was frantic, running around backstage getting all the ingredients prepped for our demo. The dark-haired CEO of the casino, Running Bear Wilson, came to the mic to introduce us to an audience that had been well oiled with all sorts of spirits served efficiently by the scantily-clad cocktail waitresses. Cute brown suede micro mini dresses with low-cut laced bodices made them look like they were wearing genuine animal skins. Too bad the trappers ran out of pelt.

When the applause died down, Ms. Tree and I walked to our table. "Gimme a hug, doll," I said and she smiled.

We started sautéing the diced onions when she said, "Tonight we're making *Spicy Venison*."

While the onions smelled tempting, my why-can't-I-filter mode took over and I said, "Even though venison is kosher, I just won't eat that shit. Last time we tried it, the hunter didn't remove all the hair. When Solly took a mouthful, he said it was like going down on me."

By the time I'd realized what I'd said, even I was shocked. Fortunately, we were in a casino where off-color comedians were second nature so the audience roared with laughter. That was all I needed to continue…

I looked at Prairie Tree, who was adding the spices before sautéing the sliced deer meat. While it was on my mind, I just had to get this one in as well…

"You know, I'm a Native Jewish American and so's my Solly. We were both born in this country. Solly's Native American name is Bouncing Dick and mine is Wet Pussy." Fortunately, Prairie Tree had a great sense of humor and started cracking up. By then, the drunks in the audience gave both of us a standing ovation.

This FannyGo Consulting was a great part-time gig. Just a few hours a week, in addition to child support payments, and I was able to take really good care of

Lori and Mitchell. David covered household and medical expenses and I covered those of the children. A few Boynton Beach excursions a year, and we were not *kvetching*.

I got into the country bumpkin lifestyle by reading the local Orange County, New York, newspaper, *The OC Chronicle*. And since I was only working part-time and the kids were in school most of the day, I had time on my hands. When I saw an ad from the newspaper's editor calling for local business owners to contribute to a business column, I figured what the hell? I'd always had a big mouth, so why not put it on paper? I emailed the business editor to apply, sending a brief description of my business and my bio.

I was hired immediately but, then again, at that time many local-yokel plumbers and feed store operators could barely write their names, let alone show an interest in writing for a newspaper. Each week, the business editor would send the few of us literate participants a business question of the week on Mondays. We had until Tuesday to reply and on Thursdays, the Biz Notes column would appear. I made sure to reply immediately so I had a better chance of making that week's edition. It was also an excellent vehicle for subtle business plugs strategically inserted within our short three- to four-sentence reply.

Thanks to Biz Notes and *The OC Chronicle*, I got my first real client, since my connection to Land and Sea Imports as a client had already been established by my having worked there for many years. Mrs. Gertie Sunstone, eighty, and her hubby, Menachem, lived in Liberty, New York, not too far away from the hallowed grounds of the 1969 Woodstock festival.

After a few weeks of contributing to Biz Notes, I got a call from Gertie. She saw from the *Chronicle* that I knew importing. She'd been trying to have her textile baking invention manufactured for over forty years without luck and knew it would be cheaper to do so in China. I knew China factories and I knew textiles. Thanks to Gertie, FannyGo Consulting launched and a few months later she had her first shipment of baking bands. The product helped layer cakes come out even on top—no cutting of tops was necessary to spread frosting.

A few press releases, courtesy of the *Chronicle*, and I began to grow a decent-sized client base. Soon, I was lecturing about importing, first to local inventor groups in the tri-state area (New York, New Jersey, and Connecticut), and then to nationwide inventor trade shows. We started out with overhead projectors and PowerPoint transparencies—funny how times have changed.

Living with David when I was twenty-two was to be quite different from when I was in my early forties. I guess I thought that I was going to have a perfect life after leaving my first marriage and reuniting with my first love.

First of all, I was inexperienced in the way of the world and knew nothing about addictions. Yes, friends—addictions. At twenty-two, I knew David liked to drink, but it never entered my mind that there might be other issues. Now, more than twenty years later, David had stopped smoking and drinking. Yes, I knew before we got back together that he used to go to Atlantic City to gamble after Elsie passed away. But why not? He was by himself and retired. But now he had a family and his Fanny, so what happened?

David took to blowing tons of money on the Internet when both online gambling and multi-level marketing schemes were in their infancy. David, Mitchell, and Lori all had desktop computers in an area off the living room near the patio, and David often forgot to close his web pages. There were online casino websites and obvious business scam sites openly displayed on his screen. "You can make a million dollars by clicking here." I was concerned but instead set my wheels spinning. Perhaps I was living with blinders on, but I loved this man, so why not try something?

As a former computer programmer, David was good in math. I suggested he take a course in tax return preparation with the long-established G&Q Bunk Company. Every year, a few months before tax season, the Bunk Company would offer free courses in an effort to recruit new tax preparers who were mostly retirees. It was a perfect job for David.

I was so happy to see him go off to work with his old, tan IBM attaché case, dressed in a shirt and tie, far away from the temptation of online gambling and online business scams. Well, that lasted just two tax seasons and when Bunk Company decided they wanted their preparers to become salespeople, David quit.

He liked the tax preparation aspect of the job, but he did not like trying to convince the customers to buy into an early concept: electronic filing. This was something that Bunk Company was initiating, though it's become routine nowadays and the cost has likely since been incorporated into the tax return preparation fee. But back then, it was an extra charge and most people just wanted to take their hard-copy return with them, walk, and mail it in by themselves.

Next came the multi-level marketing schemes. When David received a large box of blank envelopes and several pages of pre-printed adhesive labels in the mail, I asked him, "What's this about?"

In his cheerful voice, he replied, "Oh, I'm glad. I'm starting a business. All I have to do is stick these labels on the envelopes, buy some stamps, stuff this promotional information, and we're going to be rich." Ten thousand dollars is a lot of moolah for one large box with labels and envelopes. And all the recipients had to do was spend $10,000 for their own large boxes.

Oy vey.

Now, I'll admit I wasn't savvy when it came to online businesses, but by then I was operating FannyGo Consulting for a few years and it wasn't doing badly. And my common sense was, in fact, growing.

Then, towards the end of 1999, David began to pay sharp attention to the online Y2K mass email hysteria. Not only did he stockpile and fill one side of our two-car garage with survivor supplies such as canned goods, bottled water, and batteries, but he purchased them directly from the suspect sites. Every few days we'd get deliveries of merchandise that could have easily been purchased at the local ShopRite supermarket, probably for half the expense. As a former computer programmer, David really bought into all of that Y2K shit.

When January 1, 2000, arrived and nothing happened, David saw what a fool he'd been. Our computers didn't even blow up. How could such a smart man be so stupid? So the first week of January, we donated all the goodies to a food bank. We had a big tax write-off that year.

I began to see a pattern here. I attributed it to David's age and health. He was taking meds for blood pressure and acid reflux. He was diagnosed with Barrett's esophagus, a pre-cancerous condition, and had a hiatal hernia. Maybe the meds were affecting his reasoning? Boy, was I in denial. I had no experience with addictions.

And speaking of declining health, Mommy became ill in October 2000. She had already been losing her mind for the previous few years since her 1998 surgery for a fractured hip. The general anesthesia combined with her meds just didn't jive. She began to subscribe to every magazine for which she'd received a solicitation by mail. At one point, she had fifteen magazine subscriptions. Harry's wife, Karen, had to take over paying her bills because Mommy just forgot. I got fed up with the magazine subscription companies preying upon the elderly, so I threatened each and every company with legal action if they didn't stop her subscriptions.

Finally, one day in early November, Mommy called Harry—who in Yonkers lived closest to her in the Bronx—saying she didn't feel well. Harry ran over to find Mommy at the top of the steps, unable to get down the stairs, with her face swollen from an apparent lack of oxygen.

An ambulance *schlepped* her to nearby Our Lady of Mercy Hospital where she was diagnosed with pneumonia. We were clueless. She barely pulled through and had to go to rehab at the Hebrew Hospital Home in Co-op City. By then, Mommy had forgotten our names. She did smile when we visited, but that pneumonia took away the rest of her mind. Oxygen deprivation. She had to wear a motion- and location-monitoring device on her ankle.

One morning, before we visited, as the story went, she was in her wheelchair by the window in her room. Weak, she went to get up, unattended, to look out the window at the birds in the trees. She missed her parrots at home. The ankle alarm malfunctioned and she fell forward and cracked the other hip. One of the aides heard whimpering around dinner time and they rushed her to

Jacobi Hospital, famous at the time for being the armpit of the world. It was there they discovered she had a critical infection but they still wanted to operate on her broken hip.

One morning, I received a call from a surgeon who said he had spoken with my brothers. They had given him the green light to proceed with surgery.

"Your mom has sepsis, but I think it will be okay for us to go ahead and operate to fix her hip," was all he said. In 2001, Google was a little-known method for finding out about everything. I had no time to go to the library. But common sense would dictate that you don't do surgery with an infection present. Since my brothers overruled me two to one, I really had no say in the matter. I just thanked him for calling but was in shock.

Three days later, in late January 2001, exactly fourteen years after Daddy died—January was a bad month for old Jews—Jane Goldman breathed her last eighty-one-year-old's breath in the armpit of the world's shit-hole hospital. No one would have listened to Fanny Goldman, the youngest of the three Goldman children. Marty and Harry had to be in charge of this bad decision. I would like to think she might still be alive today, sitting strapped into a wheelchair, looking out a window to watch the birds. And the fucking surgeon would not have Jane's $25,000 contribution to his country club membership.

At the end of Mommy's funeral service, Marty, Harry, and I, with our spouses, walked down the aisle to the back of the chapel. In the pews to my left, I saw two of her fifty-year-long Bronx neighbors, Flo and Callie, gossiping to each other while one pointed to me, "Fanny never, *ever* visited Jane." That was not the thing to say at a funeral, especially since first, I had visited her almost every week with Lori and Mitchell, and second, they even *saw* us at Jane's house. Even though Flower, New York, was about an hour and a half away, I made sure Jane was a big part of the kids' lives. At that point, I had confirmation that Jane had lost her mind a few years before if this is what she told her old biddy neighbors. Still, it hurt me.

Now who would make my family a good chicken soup? I checked my recipe box and remembered I'd managed to score the recipe for *Grammy Jane's Jewish Penicillin* a few years back in 1998 when she still had at least some of her mind left. I finally realized why she'd ask the same question over and over again. "Why don't you ever bring the children to visit me?" she would ask whenever I'd phone her. Not, "I miss you," or "I love you," which was something she always professed to Lori and Mitchell but never to me. Of course, whenever she would ask that question it was usually a day or two after the kids and I had just visited her. But I did, in fact, have her classic recipe which she had jotted down for me in her perfect 1920s penmanship class handwriting. *Nebuch*.

It was a veritable gold mine in a *tepple* (cooking pot), an ingested bliss for those normal people, unlike myself, who ate chicken. How many non-vegetarian Jews don't eat chicken?

Let me tell you why I stopped eating chicken. In 1974, our pet parrot, who carried on rational conversations with family members, flirted with my brothers, and cursed in Yiddish, kicked the bucket. She had been in our family for over sixty years and was brought to the United States from the jungles of Panama during World War I to my mother's Austrian grandmother who lived in Poughkeepsie, New York. So basically, she was my great-grandmother's pet, my mother's pet, and my pet. I was nineteen at the time and the way Polly looked at the bottom of her cage with rigor mortis, like an Empire Kosher chicken, ruined me for any type of poultry for the rest of my days.

Okay, I never said I wasn't a whackadoodle. But this was a major obstacle to "tasting as you cooked" because there was no way in hell I was going to taste the Jewish penicillin. Luckily, David, Lori, and Mitchell were all too happy to comply.

twenty-three

The Years Flew By

$\mathbf{B}$ook tour stop: Hard Copy Booksellers in the Financial District, New York City.

Philippe Schwartz, billionaire and former owner of France's largest chain of sex toy stores—Joie de Vivre—is back in America with a cookbook of sexy treats. I can't believe what a small world this is. Back in 2002, Philippe contacted FannyGo Consulting to look into producing his Bidet Fraiche invention. It shocked the shit out of several prospective factories in China back then; it was too risqué to manufacture a portable bidet you could hook up to any faucet *après sex* (especially gay). Nowadays, that product is very much commonplace.

Au Revoir Anal Plugs, Bon Jour Cooking, Philippe's new book, got Myrna thinking we'd be perfect together for mutual book promotions.

"Are you kidding, Myrna? I worked with this *boychik* (term of endearment for "boy") more than ten years ago. But I couldn't manufacture his invention because gay sex products were taboo with Chinese factories back then. You should see what they're making these days. We'll have a blast," I told Myrna when she reached me on my cell.

Both of our books filled one of the two front windows of the bookstore on a wooden tree-like display. The other window had a big sign which read,

"Fanny and Philippe: Book Signing Today!" Gawkers who just wanted to see us but not buy our books could peek through the left window.

Reed-thin store owner, Nina Reed, with piercings on almost every visible body part, walked towards us bent over as if reading an imaginary book while standing. When she reached us, she stood straight, cracked a smile, and called everyone over to our impromptu prep station to introduce us.

"Meet Philippe Schwartz, author of *Au Revoir Anal Plugs, Bon Jour Cooking*, and Fanny Goldman, star of TV's *Fressing with Fanny* and recent author of *Fanny on Fire*!" Applause, then I grabbed the mic.

"Thanks, Nina. Philippe, it's so good to finally meet you in person. Folks, Philippe and I worked together online in my other life when I sourced new products in China. Did you ever get your Bidet Fraiche manufactured?"

"Actually, so many sex toys took off in our chain of Joie de Vivre stores throughout France that I put that project on hold. Who knows, maybe I'll open it up again one day," said the short, fiftyish, curly-blonde Philippe, wearing a pink turtleneck and tight gray skinny jeans.

"Well let's get balling," I said, as we worked the melon-ballers on the watermelon, honeydew, and cantaloupe. "Philippe, what do you call this recipe?"

"*Lost Cherry Surprise*," he said as he stirred the balled melon with mint and lemon juice and buried the maraschino cherries under all the other fruits.

"Oops, I lost my cherry," I said as some cherries slipped from my large mixing spoon onto the purple vinyl tablecloth. "I actually remember…it was to Rafael…" I continued as the audience and Philippe laughed.

Duni-B and Puff served little paper cups of the luscious dessert to those now standing in line along the aisles of the book store, waiting for us to sign their books. With my Sharpie, I signed, "Eat this! Love, Fanny."

I never thought I'd ever be organizing a Holocaust Memorial Day assembly at the very *goyishe* (Gentile; not Jewish) Flower, New York, middle school in April 2002.

I had no choice. About a month after Mitchell's December 2001 Bar Mitzvah held at Temple Bat Yam in Greenwood Lake, I was at his school helping with a bake sale. Mitchell was still coming off that bar mitzvah high where his pride in his Jewish heritage was measured in direct proportion to the money and gifts he received. And of course, he made sure to share this with any of his classmates who would listen to him.

The school was small enough for the staff, teachers, and students to know me by name. I had plenty of time to help out over the years and I was there even more often then since Mitchell had recently been diagnosed with ADHD. So I set out to prove that although he had no *zitz fleisch* (ability to sit still and pay attention; literally "sitting meat"), that he was, in fact, really smart. My frequent presence at school may have pissed off a few, but I was determined. And when Fanny is on a mission…

Of course, it took a few years but when he graduated number three in his high school class of 2007, that mission was fulfilled. After all, bribery of one hundred dollars for a ninety-five or greater average every quarter, multiplied by four quarters a year, yielded a shrewd Mitchell at least $400 per school year. Multiply that by four years of high school and Mitchell got to fly as often as he wanted back when airfares were reasonable. And you know how Mitchell loved to fly. In this case, I had a natural sense for what would work to get Mitchell to study to his full potential, limited attention span or not. Money talks.

So that day I was sitting in the cavernous lobby with my friend Mrs. Atwood, the library teacher, a former nun, and currently-married hippie grandmother, doling out cookies and muffins at the twice-annual Youth Stopping Hunger bake sale. About two hours into the sale, the principal, Dr. Carbonaro, pulled me aside and asked, "Do you have a moment?" Well, not really, dummy. It's the third of four lunch periods and all these ravenous pre-teens see are sweets for which they would be all too happy to tear your throat out if they're not permitted to purchase them. But, I let him talk.

"Mrs. Tobin," (that's the name I used in school; Goldman was for business). "I just wanted to let you know that someone drew a little swastika on Mitchell's music notebook today. I wanted you to know before it got out of control. After all, it was just a little one."

I had to process this because I have a tendency to open my big mouth and insert my foot before thinking. So I said, "What are you doing about this? And who did it?"

Dr. Carbonaro just said, "We are investigating."

With the help of Mitchell, we found out that the culprits were the son of the president of the school board and his two cohorts. This district was still as backward as the song "Harper Valley PTA" and the school superintendent refused to accept that no matter who this was, it was a *hate crime*. After all, we were only one of three Jewish families in the entire district. Was that too insignificant a number perhaps? I contemplated a lawsuit by speaking to an Orange County prosecutor, but this was still 2002, and Flower, New York, was still an unsophisticated, "Andy of Mayberry" kind of town.

So I arranged for the Simon Wiesenthal Center in New York City to provide a holocaust survivor speaker to come and talk to the entire middle school at an assembly filled with sixth through eighth graders on Holocaust Memorial Day. My mission was accomplished when Bella Kessler passed around her tattered, faded yellow cloth Star of David she had worn on her jacket as a child in the Warsaw ghetto. Her parents and baby brother perished. The entire assembly was driven to tears, Mitchell included. No more swastika cartoons, at least for that group. Do *not* fuck with Fanny.

Mitchell, Lori, and I took FannyGo Consulting on the trade show and inventor group lecture circuits beginning the summer of 2002. We traveled all over the Northeast to Connecticut, New York, New Jersey, and Pennsylvania with Mitchell and Lori handling the audio-visual equipment and passing out handouts— yes, we still used overhead transparencies for PowerPoint presentations. I soon learned how to lecture the gospel of safe Chinese manufacturing to groups large and small.

Then, during a routine annual gynecological exam in 2005, my doctor felt thyroid nodules.

"What's a thyroid nodule?" this ignorant gal asked while my doctor ordered my biopsies. Eighteen needle biopsies later, I came out with a neck temporarily looking like Frankenstein's monster and I was scheduled to have my thyroid removed in June. Diagnosis: papillary carcinoma. Surgery was followed by radioactive iodine treatment, a throat that burned on fire for a few days, and all sorts of body scans. I had to be away from my children and David for several days because I would be, well, *radioactive*.

It was summer, so it was convenient for Lori and Mitchell to fly to Tampa to spend the time with SpaceCowboy/Joe and David went to spend a week with his sister, Renée, in Pelham. I'm surprised she didn't charge him a lodging fee.

As good as new a week later, now I was a cancer survivor.

Toward the end of May 2006, we traveled to Binghamton, New York, where my all-grown-up Lori graduated with honors from the State University of New York at Binghamton with a math major and a Spanish minor.

In June 2006, I flew Lori and Mitchell out with me to Pittsburgh where I spoke at the annual National Inventors' Expo, which was and still is the United States' largest inventor trade show. Working with factories in Asia was rapidly becoming a hot topic for inventors who were learning that it was much cheaper to manufacture their new products overseas than, unfortunately, here in America. I had the information they wanted and I gave it to them.

Then, after three days at the show, we attended the awards dinner where there were medals in various categories for the inventors. I had run to the ladies' room at the swank downtown Waldorf when I heard both Lori and Mitchell screaming under the stall, "Mommy, hurry up; you're being called to the stage!" I wiped my *schnootchkie*, washed my hands as quickly as I could, and ran back to the Blue Moon Ballroom almost tripping on my purple sequined sandals.

Fanny Goldman was given the Ambassador's Award! Thank goddess I didn't have to give a speech because I was totally unprepared for this honor.

I just ran up to the stage to give a big hug to the director, Janice Larson, and to her staff of young ladies who tirelessly organized the show every year. Fanny's *punim* (face) was on two large video screens, one to the left and one to the right of center stage. I later found out that the Ambassador's Award was given every year to an inventor or a show participant who fostered good will among inventors. Holy shit!

Then, on July 15, 2006, on his seventy-fourth birthday, David peed blood.

twenty-four
They Don't Make 'Em Like That Anymore

Ellwood Timber, born Eliyahu Timberberg in Brooklyn 1935, is well known as the Big Daddy of Woodstock. Without him, the historic 1969 "three days of love and peace" festival would never have taken place. He was responsible for arranging the town permit that facilitated the gathering of a half million hippies in White Lake, New York. And the rest, as they say, is history.

Eighty-year-old Ellwood, a lofty genius, wordsmith, interior designer, and artist, has written many books on the hippie fest, his colorful gay life in New York City, and his poignant love affair with Belgian artist Alain Ehlers. His most recent one, *Always Woodstock*, was his biggest hit to date. And since his books and my *Fanny on Fire* were handled by the same publisher, Myrna and Bobby thought it might be fun to do a cooking segment with him while he was in town visiting from Miami Beach.

Ellwood and I had spoken several times on the phone and shared many emails prior to his visit to our studios, so I knew he was witty and sarcastic. And his Brooklyn accent was laced with off-color Yiddishisms which I found quite endearing.

"I'm privileged to introduce you to my friend, Ellwood Timber, without whom the 1969 Woodstock festival would not have been possible." Out walked

Ellwood, all six feet two of him, with a surprise that I immediately knew would mean trouble, but a delightful one at that. Woody Woodstock, his sweet little silky terrier pooch, was dwarfed in the arms of my guest as I immediately began to sneeze. Here we go again with dogs, I thought to myself. First, it was the twin seeing-eye dogs for the Blind Mother Truckers and now we have another unwitting allergen-donor.

"Ah-choo. Ah-choo!" Had I known Ellwood never traveled without Woody, I would have taken an extra antihistamine. "Sorry friends, but you know I'm allergic to pooches." I gave Ellwood a hug and said, in between sneezes, "So, Ellwood, what's the good word?"

"Where's the Manischewitz? I heard we're making *charoses* (a chopped apple, walnut, and sweet wine dish usually prepared for Passover) today," said Elli. He continued, "My mother, Sofia Timberberg, the old bat, used to make the worst *charoses*, so this better be good! She once gave it to our Italian next-door neighbor, Angelina. We went to her funeral in Bensonhurst three days later." I like blunt honesty.

"Here, have a sip of the Manischewitz, and I'll join you," I interrupted. "Ah-choo."

More from Ellwood, "She used to force me to eat her awful food. Her cooking sucked. And she claimed she was so poor that she walked barefoot in twenty-foot-high snow drifts across Kiev to escape getting raped by Cossacks when she was sixteen years old. She should have fucking stayed in Russia.

"The scariest memory I have of her was when she used to take me for the *schlogn kapores* (ritual of bloody sacrifice of chickens done as atonement for sins) during Yom Kippur. From the time I was a little boy, she made me sit still in the yard while the rabbi grabbed a chicken by one wing and swung it over his head until the blood splattered everywhere. I've been a vegetarian ever since." How can you not love this man? He's too much like me.

"Have another swig of Manischewitz, Ellwood," I interrupted again before our segment got too gory. "Ah-choo."

"Shit, I forgot how tasty this Manischewitz is," slurred Ellwood as we continued to chop the apples and walnuts. Woody sat like a little angel on a chair next to our table.

"So, Ellwood, tell us about sixty-nine, err, Woodstock 1969," I said. But by then both of us had far too much of the grape to make any sense. I have to say, though, I did eventually stop sneezing. The miracle of Manischewitz!

We left it at that and I went back the next day to add a close-up of the finished *charoses* and to tape a thank you to Ellwood and Woody for their visit. I also added that our viewers should buy his new book, *Always Woodstock*, for a real treat.

This can't be good. Bladder cancer. Cigarette smoking for the majority of David's adult life was a chief contributing cause according to most medical journals. What do we do now?

After first, second, and third opinion appointments with urologists in backward Orange County made each doctor shrug their shoulders with *I dunnos*, I thought it might be a good idea to consult with the chief urologist at Mount Sinai Hospital in the city. Back in 2006, I was unaware of doctor rating sites like healthgrades.com and vitals.com. Nowadays, I use them even if I need a new doctor for toenail fungus.

Dr. Horn, who was bald and, believe it or not, wore horn-rimmed spectacles, sold us a bill of goods from the first visit. The first thing he asked us about was David's insurance, which I know now was a bad sign. Then he looked at David's medical records. I made sure to bring them with us from the various Orange County doctors.

Dr. Horn said, "Well, there are two options. We can either remove his bladder and he can live with a catheter, or there's a new procedure called a neobladder which is a bit more complicated, but has had good results." That was all I had to hear since David seemed to be in shock and the decision-making was deferred to me. No mention was made, however, as to if and how far the cancer had progressed, nor of any postoperative treatment. I wish I knew then what I know now.

After we left Dr. Horn's office, I tried to do research on the procedure on the Internet and the neobladder did seem promising. However, what I didn't know was, back then it was promising for younger men whose cancer hadn't progressed as far as David's.

Gee thanks, Dr. Horn. These fucking surgeons could operate on unsuspecting victims who had great insurance and often net thousands or more per procedure. It was the same thing that killed Mommy five years earlier.

Too late, though; we scheduled the surgery, which left David with pneumonia and various other infections in Mount Sinai for three weeks—two weeks longer than he was supposed to be hospitalized. And we know now that for seniors—David was seventy-four at the time—the longer they remain hospitalized, the more dangerous it is for preying germs to take hold.

I just did the best I could, but looking back, I should have considered Memorial Sloan Kettering, a hospital that was famous for its cancer specialties. Poor David never got a chance to "use" his neobladder as he was simply too weak to make the special effort it took to learn how. So he remained with a catheter through a port in the side of his stomach until the day he died. Sorry for being so graphic, my dear readers, but it will forever irk me.

When I finally got him out of Mount Sinai, we brought him to Manor Rehab in Montgomery, New York, and that experience also almost killed him. No one monitored him there at all. I had to beg his gastroenterologist, who was one of the only professionals with a heart—aside from the nurses—to order him out of the nursing home and into the local hospital after he had lost forty pounds in just one month.

Then, the Orange County Hospital wanted to discharge him to me after two weeks when I had no experience changing dressings, nor irrigating ports and catheters with saline. And you can forget about that costly neobladder, Dr.

Horn's work of art. I took a quick, five-minute irrigation training course from a sympathetic nurse right before we left. Every two to three hours, 'round the clock, or eight to twelve times a day, every day, "in sickness and in health," I made sure David's urine flow did not get clogged. This lasted about eight weeks and I was on the verge of collapse. Finally, after New Year's Day 2007, the Veteran's Administration hospital called with an opening. I took him there and hoped for the best.

During one of my visits, David said he had something serious to discuss with me. "Muffy, you're only fifty-two and you still have a life ahead of you. So promise me that you'll find someone who'll be nice to you." I just listened and said nothing, which, as you know by now, is a monumental task for me. I held back tears. Of course, when he said this I was still fighting hard to keep him alive as long as I could.

I visited every day to scrutinize the Nazi woman doctor assigned to his case. Can you imagine that the Veteran's Administration home wanted to deny a Korean War veteran a blood transfusion which would buy him a few more days?

Dr. Nazi said, "He's going to die anyway."

I said, "You'd better arrange the transfusion or I'll go to the press." Someone had to be his voice at the VA. And Fanny's been known for her voice since she was a little brat kid.

David got that transfusion, but he continued to bleed from his port so it was just a matter of time. I told them I wanted another transfusion, but one of the social workers—I swear they all must have taken the Hitler's Henchmen 101 training course in sensitivity—said, like Dr. Nazi, "Mrs. Tobin, he just doesn't have much time left. You don't want him to suffer anymore do you?" Talk about a slap of reality right in the kisser.

After *schlepping* back and forth every day over two hours round trip for over three months, I had lost forty pounds and was worn out. I had to pause and think of my own health which I had completely neglected trying to keep David alive. And considering I had just had thyroid cancer less than two years before, I had to choose life over impending death. Who ever said life was fair?

We "celebrated" our ninth wedding anniversary on April 10, 2007. David was clearly in pain but handed me a gift which I still have today. It was a hand-written letter, in his perfect penmanship I had grown to love, thanking me for taking care of him and for loving him. I broke down but ran out of the ward because I didn't want him to see me so distraught. When I came back, I just said I had to run to the potty or there would have been a puddle on the floor. He laughed.

A few weeks later, when I visited on a Thursday afternoon, I brought him the only thing he asked for: Coca-Cola with ice and a straw. He had gradually stopped eating a few days before and the VA facility served just a shitty, warm RC Cola in a can that would not quench David's thirst. He said it tasted like the worst grade of motor oil. Coke on ice with a straw: Fanny's final and ultimate way to feed her beloved. *Anything* for David…

As I arrived, he sat propped upright in bed in a morphine haze, but his eyes followed me as I spoke to him. He had been spiking a fever for the past week or so, so I was sure the ice would be soothing.

"*Tahteleh* (little father; a Jewish term of endearment), have a sip. Come wet your whistle." And he did. I chose to believe he would live as long as he drank the Coke, kind of like my version of "drinking the Kool-Aid." Then he took my hand and kissed it. I wasn't ready to let go, but that would be his last kiss.

He died the next morning, on April 27, 2007, fortunately feeling no pain, on a merciful dose of morphine. I became numb by osmosis, as if the morphine left David's veins and entered mine. Along with him, he took my heart. I was unwilling to let go of this man who had been in and out of my world, yet a part of my dreams and a huge part of my life for the past thirty years.

Now I had no heart and no thyroid. How could I live?

twenty-five

It's Raining Men, Redux

Solly and I were packing for another stop on my book tour. Solly insisted that his CPAP machine didn't count as a carry-on item. He said that the TSA calls it a medical device. This immediately set the gears spinning in my brain again, at full speed, quite like the rapid idea flashes I experience during my nighttime bouts with insomnia.

In my case, my brain has a shortcut connection to my mouth. I have no filter, so I looked at Solly, smiled, and asked, "What about my Rabbit vibrator? Does that count as a medical device?"

A big old grin hit Solly's *punim*, kind of typical of a man who knows he's going to get some soon.

Solly countered in his typical deadpan fashion without missing a beat, "No, *mameleh*, what you have is a dangerous weapon."

"What the fuck are you talking about?" I asked in my typical ladylike Bronx fashion.

Said Solly, "You could hijack the plane with that thing. Just pack it in your large purple spinner if you can't be without it for a few days." I laughed.

Solly continued, "But if you ask me like a nice girl, I'll be sure to let you use something that's been a part of me all my life. And the *mohel* (ritual person, often a rabbi, who provides Jewish circumcisions) made it very pretty for me when I was just eight days old." Solly takes such good care of me.

David's funeral, with military honors, would be the next to the last time I would have to see Renée, who glared at me as if his death were my fault. *Listen, you cunt. If he hadn't had me as his advocate at the VA nursing home, he'd have died a lot sooner.* But I didn't bother saying anything. I kept my mouth shut out of respect for David's mom, Patty, who was by then in her mid-nineties and in a wheelchair. The very last time I'd have to deal with Renée's bullshit attitude was at the unveiling of David's headstone at the Flower, New York, veteran's cemetery several months later.

This Fanny never did do well solo. After about a month of mourning, it was time to find a man. My survivor—and high-priced call girl—instincts kicked in almost immediately. What could I do with little money and a big house? I had no time to grieve because I knew the bills would soon pile up. Besides, I did my grieving in the last few months of David's life when we realized his bladder cancer had far passed the curable stage and had metastasized throughout his body.

There was no Intro by Camera to turn to. They had long been out of business. And besides, *schlepping* to White Plains with no heart and no thyroid wouldn't be wise even *if* they were still in business.

By 2007, I was fairly computer literate and had heard about a relatively new phenomenon that replaced the ancient twentieth-century video-dating. Online dating was becoming the newest way for singles of all ages to meet.

I searched and found meet-a-jew.com, jewishmagnetism.com, and jewsenior.com. Lori and Mitchell urged me to be careful, so they helped me complete my online profiles. But they both felt it was too soon. They just didn't understand. I *needed* to find someone.

My first date as a widow was with Rob Asher whom I met for a nice lunch at the Riverside on the Hudson in Newburgh, New York. He was handsome, sixtyish, with a gray beard. He was divorced but made it quite clear that he never planned on remarrying. Next.

Then there was John McFarland—not Jewish—who was an elementary school teacher. He took me out to dinner on our first date and seemed normal enough. On our second date, we went to the Orange County Fair and then to the Orange County drive-in movie theatre afterwards. However, during *The Simpsons Movie* he unzipped his fly, whipped it out, and said, "Why don't you kiss this?"

So as I opened the car door, I said, "Why don't you kiss *this*?" as I mooned him and then ordered a cab from the pay phone at the drive-in refreshment stand. And *this* was allowed to be around children in a classroom every day?

The next date was a gastronomical delight for Fanny the foodie. I met Jim Santacroce, a widower from Peekskill, New York, at the Culinary Institute of America in Hyde Park. We took a tour of the various cooking classes and then enjoyed a delicious and classy lunch prepared and served by CIA students. After our date, he kissed my cheek and asked if he could call me again. Well, two weeks later he did and said he was moving to Puerto Rico.

Then I met Roy Adler, later to be known as the Pig Man. Roy, who was Jewish, was living part-time in a rodent-infested old country apartment in rural Phoenicia, New York, and part-time on the north shore of Long Island. The part-time residence on Long Island was an easy commute for when he worked Mondays through Wednesdays as a doorman at the Helmsley Park Lane Hotel in the city.

Though he was short and round, I liked his brains and he was good in the hay. But he was a bleeping liar. Yes, folks, we were together on and off for almost three years, from 2007 through 2010. I found out that, although his profile indicated he was divorced, he was, in fact, still married to the mother of his two grown sons. She lived in their house on Long Island. He made sure he didn't spill this minor detail until we were already quite fond of each other and had already been intimate. I had clearly spelled out my choice for either divorced or widowed men as I did not check the married or separated boxes on the dating website.

"But I'm going to get a divorce," he insisted. It was Yom Kippur—the Day of Atonement—so I wondered how he'd planned to atone for this convenient lie. This brought me back to my seventeen-year-old self with Rafael Aldana in the Bronx, also married. Sure, you're going to get a divorce.

Well, he eventually did, but that was two years later when his wife could no longer stand his philandering. In the settlement, she won the house on Long Island but by then he had already bought a house in rural Orange County and several pens of pigs. A kosher pig farmer? I think not.

"I moved here for you, Fanny." Gee thanks. Like I wanted to visit or even live in a country house that reeked of pig shit when the summer wind blew through the back yard and in through the open windows. And it seemed that the mice followed him from Phoenicia to his new house when I saw the gnawed-through toilet paper rolls under the bathroom sink. Mice, mosquitoes, pig shit, and no air conditioning await you in your palace, Princess Fanny.

By 2010, even though I still occasionally saw Pig Man—but only if he came to *my* house—I had already begun to date a few other guys. At one point, there was Roy number one (the Pig Man) and Roy number two (a nice guy from New Jersey), and my girlfriends used to kid me to make sure I didn't mix them up in emails. Well, all it took was one time and I lost Roy number two by sending him the wrong email.

Then I met Dan the Customs Man. Since I was a licensed customs broker and saw on his profile page that he was a retired customs agent, I thought we might have something in common. Except when I found out that he liked to dress up in his old customs agent uniform, which was several sizes too small, and wanted me to role play as a Russian spy he was arresting—complete with handcuffs. Poor guy; diabetes had rendered him impotent, but he never gave up trying.

I met Baron Rosenzweig, from Albany, during the summer of 2010. He was a perfect gentleman who took me to all the finest restaurants. But along with the chivalrous exterior went an obsession with oral sex. One way only—and, no, he would not reciprocate. Geez.

In August 2010, my good friend Peggy, who lived in Sullivan County—I had met her a few years back when I was covering a magazine story about her family's boutique—told me about a guy she wanted me to meet. I remember her telling me about a few dates she had been on with Raymond Holland whom she met at a temple singles' dinner group.

"Fanny, he's a cheapskate, but I know for a fact that he really wants to get married. Do you want to meet him?" asked Peggy.

"What the hell," I said.

By then I had finally dumped the Pig Man after three years when I went into my office one morning—he usually arose way before I did—and found his dating profile open with another woman's photo and correspondence in broad daylight on my computer.

Peggy introduced me to Raymond Holland and he was almost seventy-five. I had promised myself that David would be the only much older man I'd ever be with, but he was already gone over three years and I still needed to find a man. Money was tight. Well, Raymond was nice, fairly attractive, and definitely cheap. So I made sure when we went out, that we didn't go to cheap places. Nice restaurants and theatre, if you please.

During one moment of passion, Raymond told me he loved me and wanted to marry me. He earned a good living as a court stenographer—yes, he was still working at seventy-four—so I seriously had to consider this. Either I would sell my house in Flower or he'd have to sell his house in Sullivan County, New York, where he'd lived for over forty years. But soon the red flags began to surface. First, he was a hoarder, which probably was the reason why he'd lived in the same home for over forty years. He had so much shit in it, piled in some rooms from floor to ceiling, that he'd have trouble knowing where to begin sorting and getting rid of the stuff.

Apparently, he told his three children we would be getting married. Of course, I hadn't yet said yes, so I was caught off guard when I got a phone call one Saturday when I was preparing for our date.

"Hi, this is Lauren Holland, Raymond's daughter, and you're on a conference call with my brother Dale and my sister Andrea."

"Yes," I said, wondering why they didn't say something nice like, "Happy to meet you," or, "We're glad you're keeping company with our dad."

"We just want you to know that if you marry our dad, we'll sue you for our inheritance if you try to fight for it." I slammed down the phone, my whole body shaking with anger. Why the fuck did Raymond give them my phone number? He was on his way, so I'd find out.

It was a warm October afternoon, so I had left the garage door open and he knew he'd be able to find me working in my upstairs office. Flower was still a safe town. In walked Raymond with a big smile on his face. He pointed downward and said, "Look what I brought you, Fanny."

What is it with *that* generation of men and their dicks?

I replied, "What're you doing, hanging it out for air?" Apparently, he unzipped and whipped it out downstairs thinking I'd jump on it when he arrived upstairs. This guy was clearly becoming senile, so now I understood why his kids ganged up on me—to protect their share in Daddy's money. But they didn't have to worry. I asked Raymond to leave after I told him about his rude, disrespectful children. And after that, I changed my online profile to read that I would only date *widowers without children*. That could further narrow my options, but I had to take a chance. I seriously thought of adding "who kept it in their pants unless asked nicely to remove,, but stopped myself.

There were two more guys on the scene before I finally met the love of my life, Solly. Never-married Randall Hibner, cute enough, had *schlepped* all the way down from Portland, Maine, to meet me. I told him I only dated widowers, but he insisted on making the trip. He wanted me to come and live in his unfinished log cabin. "We only have mice when it gets cold." Yup, I'm on the first train *not* to Portland, Maine. As you must know by now, Fanny is scared shitless of mice.

Then, Dalton Norris—radical convert to Judaism who went to temple practically every waking moment—seemed like a possibility. Tall, sandy-haired, and a few years older, he was retired and lived in Greenville on the other side of Orange County. He was, in fact, a widower with no children. But it lasted only a few months because I went with him once to the conservative services for Rosh Hashanah and after several hours, I fell asleep. Those were some *long* services. I love the Jewish culture and traditions, but I just can't do organized religion.

So in the meantime, with time on my hands, right before I met Solly, I wrote two books on product safety and working with factories in China. It was good therapy and I continued on the inventor group lecture circuit, traveling throughout the country whenever I could.

I can't believe it, but it seems like I dated more with the online dating sites after David's death than I did back in the seventies when I did the video dating. This went on and off until I met Solly that wonderful night in December 2011.

twenty-six

When Fanny Met Solly

A girl walks into a bar. Actually, it was Chili's in Butler, New Jersey, on Route 23. December 10, 2011: After years of those online disasters, I got a good feel for this date. Actually, *he* got a *really* good feel—of my ass, that is—but that's later on.

So there was meetthisjew.com, J-fate.com, tryrmatch.com. If a dating site existed in 2011, I tried it. Except those that were clearly porn or bestiality oriented. No S&M or blindfolds for Fanny, thank you very much. After all those losers, as I said, I updated my personal statement to read "widower only with no kids.. I had no desire to deal with anyone else's grown—and inheritance-hungry—children. Sorry, but I'm not going to lie to you.

I decided to give seniormagnetism.com one last shot since this *maideleh* (girl, usually Jewish) was not meant to be alone. I loved my men and I loved being able to wrap my legs around some kosher sausage at night. Loneliness is not for sissies!

With all the men I dated after David's passing in 2007, I knew by now exactly who and what I was looking for. I completed yet another online profile, which I already knew by heart, and I remembered to specify, "If you snore, you must use a CPAP. No more room-shaking loud vibrations of the male nose-throat variety, though old-fashioned vibrators with new batteries are permissible." That would get quite a bit of attention.

Now, let's get back to that memorable day in December 2011. I spotted Solly Rabinowitz at the door from his online photo, still wearing his nerdy Bluetooth earpiece, which he eventually removed once he realized his GPS had already told him, "You have arrived at your destination."

He smiled and said, "Hi.. Then I smiled when he added, "I've been looking to do someone like you all my life!" I wasn't even the slightest bit fazed by this remark. Remember, I had to deal with guys coming for a visit with their *schlongs* (slang for penis, or "dick") hanging out of their pants and one-way oral fetishes.

I was quite ready with a retort. "Your life ain't over yet, *dahlink*!" We had communicated quite a bit by email for about two weeks before, so I knew he was a widower who had no kids. This had already given him brownie points. "It's about to be a very interesting ride," I said as we were seated.

Saul "Solly" Rabinowitz, who was voted most likely to be a wallflower in his senior year at Toms River (New Jersey) High, had no problem spilling what was on his mind, courtesy of ten years of intensive Toastmaster's International training. I hoped I'd be able to keep up with him. A twice-Rutgers grad— bachelor of arts in mathematics and master of science in computer science—he automatically got a 4.0 in Nerds in New Jersey 101.

While the cleavage-bearing, short-skirted hostess led us to our seats, I thought, how cool is that? He didn't take his eyes off me once. Besides, he'd soon learn I could provide him with all the fantasies he'd ever need.

Solly ordered the chicken tortilla soup and chicken fajitas, none of which I could sample because remember, dear friends, that Fanny doesn't eat chicken. I had the shrimp fajitas. I just sat back and let Solly do most of the talking because it seemed like he needed to and I figured, what better way to learn about someone?

Besides, I was enjoying my dinner and right now I needed my mouth to chew. I was sure I'd figure out what to do with my mouth later on if we made it to a second date.

Solly was quite subtle when, while we were taking a break from stuffing our faces, he said, "You know, I always bring my CPAP machine with me when I travel." Bingo—that took care of one of my requirements without my even having to ask. That showed me that Solly read and paid attention to my online profile.

But I never expected by far the strangest coincidence that just about sealed the deal then and there. Solly knew I lived way up in Flower, New York, and I knew he lived in central New Jersey which was why we arranged to meet mid-point in Butler, New Jersey for our first date. During dinner, I mentioned I was born in the Bronx, and Solly said, "So was I."

"Where?" I asked.

"In Westchester Square Hospital," said Solly.

"Are you fucking kidding me?" I asked, thinking I might have inadvertently included this info in my online profile. Do you know how many hospitals there are in the Bronx? This was too weird a coincidence for a lifelong Jersey boy. We proceeded to share our stories…

Mindy Rabinowitz lived in Toms River, New Jersey, with her husband, Elijah, and their two children, Delilah, six, and Dennis, two. She was expecting her third child in June 1951. Mindy wasn't due for two weeks so she decided to leave Delilah and Dennis with her mom, *Bubbe* Iris, and take a quick overnight trip up to the Bronx to visit with cousins.

Well, Mindy did arrive safe and sound at Cousin Ethel's in the Parkchester section of the Bronx; but after a delicious lunch of spicy *kishka* (beef intestine casing stuffed with flour or matzo meal, spices, and chicken fat) and *kasha varnishkes* (a buckwheat grain dish with noodles and spices), she went into labor.

Those contractions started out so close together that she missed the option of returning home to Toms River to her one-obstetrician farming community. Back then, it was kind of like a one-horse town.

The closest hospital was—you guessed it—Westchester Square Hospital and Saul P. Rabinowitz was born there on June 1, 1951. Back then, they kept new moms in the hospital for one week to recuperate from scopolamine-assisted labor, or "twilight sleep,, as it used to be called. Not like today when, with an uncomplicated childbirth, one's medical insurance—*if* she is fortunate enough to have medical insurance—barely covers an overnight stay.

Mindy wasn't going anywhere for seven days, so she pondered a middle name for little Solly whose first name, Saul, was after Shmuel, Mindy's late father. It was a Jewish tradition and honor to name after a deceased relative. Elijah, a chicken farmer, couldn't get relief for the daily work involved in tending to his coops until Solly was three days old. That's when he would finally get to meet his third child.

There were no televisions in hospitals back then and Mindy, by that point, was bored to tears after reading the sole copy of an old *Ladies' Home Journal* the previous new mom had left in the room cover-to-cover seven times. There was an article about another new mom from Phoenix who created twenty different recipes using red snapper. That story, in turn, reminded Mindy of her favorite trip to Phoenix, Arizona, where she and Eli went on their honeymoon. That was it: Phoenix.

A few days after Solly's birth, the records clerk at Westchester Square Hospital stopped by Mindy's bedside to ask about her new son's name for the birth certificate. The clerk, Kelly O'Sullivan, had a thick Irish brogue even though she spoke like she had just had her adenoids removed. You see, she was deaf, wore two hearing aids, and had Coke bottle eyeglasses. But she had been hired immediately without even an interview, because on her résumé she claimed she typed ninety words per minute. No one even bothered to give her a typing test on the hospital's sole ancient Remington typewriter. Westchester Square Hospital was in the midst of a population explosion and the previous clerk, who only typed thirty words per minute, was so overworked that she quit in 1946, just as post-war women began to spit out boomer rugrats in record volume.

The chief obstetrician-gynecologist with privileges at the hospital was a dreamy, young Dr. Percival (Percy) Nussbaum, also known as Dr. Pussy, who bore a strong resemblance to the hunk fifties actor William Holden. The story goes that a good number of young Bronx gals chose to get knocked up just so they could look at Dr. Pussy in between their legs once a month for the duration of their pregnancies.

And once a week, the good doctor just signed off on a stack of birth certificates while Kelly O'Sullivan serviced him under his desk. Dr. Pussy never checked names while he autographed those documents because he was clearly concentrating on other more urgent matters.

So here I was, three years later, in 1954, the only girl and last child of Jane and Michael Goldman. My first name came from Daddy Michael's deceased Aunt Faygeleh. Mommy Jane decided on a more American-sounding Fanny instead of Faygeleh. The first initial would suffice, and I'm glad it did, because as I got older I learned that Faygeleh was literally "bird" in Yiddish but was also Yiddish slang for "faggot,, a not-nice street vulgarity in those days.

A full seven days at Westchester Square Hospital for Mommy was like a vacation away from caring for two active little boys, Marty and Harry, who were seven and a half and five at the time. The story goes that one of the neighbors came by for a visit and brought her a clematis plant. Mommy loved the pretty pink and purple flowers. She, like Mindy three years before, had plenty of time on her hands during that week to think of middle names because my first name was non-negotiable. Otherwise, according to tradition, dead Aunt Faygeleh's soul would forever go ambling about the earth without a namesake. So this would be my name: Fanny Clematis Goldman. Or so it was believed.

Jane was so sleep-deprived in the first several weeks of being Mommy to now three children, including a newborn with excellent lungs, that she never bothered to open up the envelope with the return address marked "Bureau of Vital Records.. She labeled it "Fanny's birth certificate" in her careful 1920s penmanship and filed it away inside the black and white serving table where she kept all of the family records and photos, in the teeny six-by-eight-foot dining room.

Until, that is, when it was time for me to apply for my learner's permit to drive in 1971. Cami accompanied me to the DMV, and when I handed over that same, seventeen-year-old envelope, Cami looked at the clerk and all of a sudden there were stereo belly laughs as I stood there mortified. My birth certificate, thanks to Kelly O'Sullivan and Dr. Pussy, proved my identity as Fanny Clitoris Goldman. So that was how I got the nickname "The Clit," which ultimately served me well once I was old enough to appreciate it.

But that's not all. Three years earlier, in Toms River, New Jersey, Mindy Rabinowitz, now well-rested with little Solly who was, and still is a talented sleeper, had her mom to help out with the two older children. After Delilah brought in the mail a few weeks after Solly was born, Mindy opened up the envelope with the return address from the Bronx, New York, planning to file Solly's birth certificate in the same shoebox with Delilah's and Dennis's.

She let out a whoop that woke up little Solly in the bassinet way at the other end of the house while *Bubbe* Iris came hobbling with Delilah and Dennis on each hand, to find Mindy laughing hysterically. Luckily, Mindy had a wonderful sense of humor.

"*Vus machst du, mameleh?* (What are you doing little Mommy? What's happening?)" asked *Bubbe* Iris.

Mindy said, in between chuckles, "His name is Saul Penis Rabinowitz!" *Bubbe*, with limited English, had a puzzled look on her face; but Delilah and Dennis clearly knew the names for boy and girl genitalia. So that is how little Solly bore the nickname of "Pee Pee" practically until he got to Rutgers. Of course, Mindy and Elijah ultimately got the birth certificate corrected with Solly's middle name changed to Phoenix, but it wasn't until much later.

After hundreds of complaints, Westchester Square Hospital bade farewell to Kelly O'Sullivan who ultimately became Mrs. Dr. Pussy in 1955.

A snappy December wind bit at our faces as we sprinted out to the Chili's parking lot. "This ain't Boca," I said. Strangely enough, in such a big parking lot, we found that our cars were parked right near each other.

Solly said, "Would you like to get together again soon? I already have a date for New Year's Eve. It's a square dance and I don't even like the gal, but a commitment's a commitment."

It was refreshing to find someone who made good on a promise. I replied, "I also made a date for New Year's Eve, but sure, let's decide on another time." I thanked him for dinner and gave him a hug and a peck on the cheek. Solly returned the favor with a nice bear hug and grabbed my ass for a quick feel.

Good, I thought, this guy has *chutzpah* (guts, balls, nerve). Little did I know that within a few weeks we'd be engaged and planning a wedding. After all, we already had that Westchester Square Hospital connection, and with that, we knew it was *bashert* (meant to be; destiny).

twenty-seven

Truth Be Told

Esther-Chanah Lieberman, the wunderkind chef of Noshes, a chain of California eateries, is due for a segment on *kugels*, or puddings, on today's show. With all of Solly's and my wedding preparations, I didn't have time to Google search her like I normally would when I prepare for my guests. So Mandiyee already briefed me on Ms. Lieberman's specialties and cooking style while Duni-B and Puff readied the set. Myrna and Bobby said she's a charming, bi-racial young Jewish woman with a quick wit and risqué sense of humor. They envisioned an Abbott and Costello "Who's on first?"-type segment, since Bobby said, "You both obviously have big mouths and share a warped sense of humor."

Myrna said that we would be preparing Esther-Chanah's *Kalifornia Kugel*, a bread pudding with pears, pecans, and raisins, made from stale multi-grain bread. There was one important thing, however, that neither Mandiyee, nor Myrna, nor Bobby told me.

"And now, peeps, please welcome Esther-Chanah Lieberman, whiz-kid and owner of Noshes, a well-known franchise of West Coast cafés known for simple and tasty Jewish cooking." This young woman in front of me is full-figured, about my height, has brown skin and dark brown, curly, shoulder-length hair which she wears wrapped by a single braid in a low ponytail. She is clearly bi-racial, but wait. *She has my face.* She looks just like me and she looks just like Lori.

Then it hit me. My eyes immediately bugged out, I opened my mouth wide, and it started to freeze into what seemed like a permanent, *"Oy!"*

Esther-Chanah said, *"Mameleh!"*

With tape rolling and tears flooding our eyes, we embraced like we were trying to make up for thirty-five years in one brief segment.

Bobby slapped her knee, swooped a shocked, normally tight-assed Myrna up for a big, wet kiss, and said, "Hot damn! Our ratings just jumped off the charts."

I knew it right away. This is my firstborn. But just as we heard, "Cut," so Zsa-Zsa could rush in and touch up our wet, runny makeup, we saw Freddy collapse and fall forward from his chair next to one of the cameras.

Holy shit! What the fuck's going on today? Poor Freddy! Fortunately, stocky Bobby was right next to him so she was able to cushion his fall and prevent him from landing on his face. Freddy was unconscious when Dr. Edelstein—you remember our red-headed studio doctor who stitched up my middle finger—rushed out with Carlos, our portly drag queen stagehand who today was dressed in a lavender toga. They managed to lift Freddy onto a gurney bound for Dr. Edelstein's backstage office.

My knees were shaking while I watched as Myrna—cool, calm, and collected—called Tina and asked her to get down to the city as soon as she could and said that Freddy was in capable hands. It was almost like everyone other than I expected something to happen to Freddy by now and they were more prepared than a Marine Corps silent drill platoon. After all, this was my old boyfriend and nothing could happen to him. Talk about denial.

So, my *fraynds* (friends), I wasn't entirely forthright with you. Right at the time I met Boris Perlmutter that fateful night at the Jewish singles dance with Sara Ornstein in New York City at the end of 1979, I had a one-night stand with a tall, sexy, brilliant man. Mack Sabatino had called me to say that someone had picked my tape and he had to follow protocol to notify me even though his profile wasn't necessarily within my selection criteria.

"Malik Sharif is a black history professor at Pace University," said Mack. Did I want to come in and view Malik's tape? Hmmm...the name sounded mysterious—almost exotic—sort of like Omar Sharif, the gorgeous Egyptian actor who nailed the very Jewish Barbra Streisand's Fanny Brice character in *Funny Girl.*

I wasn't dating anyone in particular at that moment—and that was maybe for like three seconds, because when wasn't Fanny dating someone?—so I went to White Plains to watch Malik's tape. There I viewed a black man whose dark eyes with long, curly lashes seemed to be speaking directly to me. I was mesmerized and during the videotape, when he said he loved Jewish deli food and Jewish women, that did it. Mack gave him my number and when he called I thought I'd be meeting a black history professor. Maybe he could tell me all about the Black Panthers, Malcolm X, Rosa Parks, and Angela Davis? And maybe I'd learn first-hand why the girls in my Bronx 'hood always used to say, "Once you've gone black, you can never go back."

When we met during Christmas-New Year's week at the Rye Ridge Deli (after all, he loved Jewish deli food), we got to talking over corned beef on rye with Russian and two *kasha knishes.* I asked him about his Black History classes. There and then I looked like a complete fool when Malik chuckled and told me that Mack Sabatino always got that wrong.

"Well," said Malik with a deep, sing-song voice in between bites of his *knish. Oy*, I felt like he was eating *my knish*. "I am *obviously* black, and I *am* a history professor. But I'm not a Black History professor," he said while a dollop of Russian dressing lined his upper lip.

I licked my upper lip as if to signal to him to wipe it off. But Malik just said, "Ooh, baby, do that again!" as I processed my obvious, overt signal. When it hit me, I just laughed.

It was kind of a letdown because I was looking for some sort of juicy stories to tell my girlfriends. But he did tell me he changed his name from Malcolm Smith because the Jewish women he dated all seemed to enjoy, in a perverse way, the look on their mothers' faces when they mentioned they were dating a black, history professor named Malik Sharif. It's all where you put the comma.

I had on a low-cut silver lamé top and tight, black bell-bottom pants. At twenty-five, I looked damn fetching. Malik kept on staring at my braless cleavage in between bites of knish washed down with Dr. Brown's Diet Cream Soda. It was getting late and I had to go to work the next day, so I figured what the heck—I had never tasted the dark meat, so why not give it a try?

The very second we got into my third-floor walk-up, we started making out like teenagers in the back seat of a '57 Chevy at a drive-in movie. Since I had an IUD, HIV wasn't even an issue in 1979, *and* this man was a professor (how naïve was I back then?) this would all be safe, right? Wrong! So, getting back to where I said my story about Boris Perlmutter wasn't exactly true—what was, in fact, true was that I did get pregnant while using an IUD. I had been using one for at least five years by that point, so I never had any thoughts that there might be an "oops.

I sensed that Malik did love his Jewish women, but also loved his freedom and would forever remain a bachelor, so he divulged during some post-coital small talk. I knew I wanted to get married—the sooner the better—so my one-night stand was just that. It was fun, it was delicious, but it would never be anything beyond that.

Within a few days, Sara Ornstein and I were heading to the city for the holiday season Jewish singles dance where I would meet Perlmutter. Most of the rest of what I already told you about him was true, but for some reason, he always insisted on using a condom even though I told him I had an IUD. Probably for the same reason he wiped his wee-wee with toilet paper after he peed. Besides, HIV wasn't to become a disastrous news topic until the early eighties. Nonetheless, after several weeks and a missed period, I did find out I was most definitely with

210

child.

All the things I told you about Perlmutter were true, and we were together for several months. The fact that I would not abort the child drove him away and we did break up before the baby was born. He just did not want children, at least back then. Funny thing was, I saw him from a distance about ten years later in Larchmont, New York, at a street carnival when Lori was about six and Mitchell about two, holding the hands of two small children who looked just like him. He was accompanied by a short Hispanic woman. Glad he didn't see me, because I didn't want to get into updating him on the following truth...

I stayed working at Chemical Commodities until I was due to give birth. My boss, Mendel, was sympathetic and understanding. I lived with Mommy and Daddy in the Bronx during the last week of my pregnancy and I knew I was giving up this baby for adoption. Mommy was less than thrilled because she loved babies. But my parents knew better than to go against Fanny, especially when my hormones were raging.

On October 12, 1980, at Misericordia Hospital in the Bronx, I gave birth to a perfect, seven-pound baby girl with dark brown, curly hair and milk chocolate skin, who was, without a doubt, the daughter of Malik Sharif. I was certainly not going to try to notify him as he made it clear he would be a lifelong bachelor. I could not handle a fatherless baby. I could not keep this precious gift.

I had already signed a contract for a direct adoption through the Levinson Agency, the same agency Mommy used during the early 1950s when she and Daddy were foster parents. There was a long gap between Harry (1949) and me (1954), so Mommy used her time productively caring for out-of-wedlock Jewish babies until she became pregnant with me.

After a few days in the hospital, I was back home and soon back to work. I did identify Malik Sharif on the birth certificate as the father. Although the adoption records were closed and there was no Internet back then, I did ultimately find out that my little bundle was given to two Holocaust survivors who couldn't have children of their own due to the perverse Dr. Mengele and his demonic experiments. As horrific as this whole experience was for me, it did my heart good to know that my little girl went to two deserving parents. Somehow, I just knew she would be loved...

So although I never forgot about this little girl and from time to time wondered where she was, especially as every October 12 would pass, Lori and Mitchell filled the void that was created by the loss of my firstborn. And now I didn't have to go far because life had come full circle and Esther-Chanah Lieberman was back in our lives.

Back in my dressing room, Esther-Chanah introduced me to my first grandchild, Leah-Shira, a brown-skinned little beauty who also shared our faces.

"Is this my new *Bubbe*?" asked this sweet little girl as she looked at her mommy.

Esti shook her head yes, as we both immediately melted into a blubber of tears. And I was crying not only tears of joy, but also tears of concern for my dear Freddy, who was rushed to NYU Medical Center. Dr. Edelstein thought he had a stroke, but let's wait for the tests results.

In turn, Leah-Shira started to cry so I resorted to what I do best. I feed my flock when they are sad. Matter of fact, in my role as a Jewish mother, I feed them for no reason at all. I always have *nosherei* (snacks) in my dressing room. And distraction for little ones has always worked for me. "Come, *mameleh*, how'd you like a nice piece of *rugelach*?"

Zeeseleh (little sweetness) put one hand on her hip, tilted her chin, and said with attitude, "Thank you, but I only like apricot. This looks like raspberry. Mommy says I'm 'lergic to raspberry." A true Jewish girl, my granddaughter.

Zeeseleh, which has become my nickname for her, was born in 2011 with an anonymous sperm donor father. Of course, I later found out that with all the work that was involved in building up her many West Coast cafés, Esti simply didn't have time for a relationship. Kids these days! But she desperately wanted to give her aging adoptive parents, Rose and Herschel Lieberman, a grandchild. That would be her ultimate gift to them for giving her such a wonderful life. And did they *kvell* (to beam with pride) over their little granddaughter! Unfortunately, Rose passed away in 2013 and Herschel a year later in 2014.

So almost immediately after Herschel's passing, Esther-Chanah decided it was time to try to find her birth parents. And goddess bless the Internet. Professor Malcolm Smith—apparently he reverted back to his birth name sometime in the 1990s—had passed away in 2009. But she did manage to see some pictures of him from a few of Pace University's alumni publications. It's all good.

twenty-eight
Never Tote Chicken Soup to a Jewish Wedding

I've been spending a lot of time online looking for a rabbi to perform our wedding ceremony. Yes, Solly and I are getting married! I told you, it was *bashert*. Besides, wouldn't you think that two sixty-somethings would know what they want when they found it after hunting around for several years?

Hour after hour on jewtietheknot.com, and I'd finally narrowed it down to a few rabbis whose websites had nice photos and engaging résumés. Solly and I decided we wanted to meet with a rabbi who lived in Passaic, New Jersey, and made an appointment to interview him on Sunday, March 24, at two p.m.

Rabbi Moses Seinfeld was an interfaith rabbi who, according to his website, had performed gay civil ceremonies, marriages between Christians and Jews, and traditional Jewish marriages. Heck, he even performed so-called marriages between barnyard animals whose fairly odd human parents were put off by their pet sheep's constant humping, so they sought out the services of Rabbi Moses hoping their sheep's deed-doings might be sanctified.

Solly had his trusty GPS phone app all programmed and away we went. As the GPS told us, "You have arrived at your destination. Your destination is on your right," we immediately started combing through our wedding notebook to check the address. Two-forty-nine Church Street: check. Those *were* the numbers on the front of the cozy looking brick house in the center of the block. But wait. There were strings of green Saint Patrick's Day shamrocks decorating all around the front of the house. Hold on. There was a prominent cement Virgin Mary statue with a floral halo in the right corner of the fenced in yard. Um, wasn't it about to be Passover?

Just as Solly and I began to panic and re-check our notebook, then double check the GPS, out walked a tall, handsome man with graying hair from a side entrance to his house. He waved at us and shouted, "Solly, Fanny, is that you? I'm Rabbi Moses! Come on in!" WTF?

We followed the rabbi to his study at the rear of his home. Still unsure we were in the right location—maybe he was renting an office?—we let him do the talking. "So everyone wonders about the Virgin Mary statue and our seasonal Christian decorations in the front of our house. You see, my wife is Catholic..." Who ever heard of a rabbi marrying a Catholic girl?

"So, this beauty and I met online—at seniormagnetism.com to be specific," said Solly as he put his arm around me. Then I began to speak about the type of wedding ceremony we were looking for. We shared our personal lives and began to feel quite comfortable with him. Moses was born into a Hasidic, ultra-orthodox family. His mother was bipolar. Can you imagine? Not a half hour into our first meeting and he was pouring his heart out to us about his whackadoodle mom. I liked this dude.

When he was seventeen, he left Orthodox Borough Park, Brooklyn, and went to live with cousins in Passaic, New Jersey, who were Reform Jews—like night and day. After studying to become an accountant, he met the love of his life who was none other than a Catholic girl, a *shikse*. Fast forward a few years: they were planning on marrying in the early eighties and could not find anyone to perform an interfaith ceremony. A big light bulb flashed in front of Moses' eyes as he thought, "It must be easier for love to prevail!" And then and there, he decided to study to be a Reform rabbi with a specialty in interfaith weddings.

Now, of course we didn't need him for an interfaith wedding so we were assured when he reiterated that he did perform traditional Jewish weddings as well.

About halfway through our nice talk, a short, brunette, middle-aged lady walked into the study with a tray of coffee, tea, and Passover cookies. Maybe it's the maid? She introduced herself.

"I'm Mary, Rabbi Moses's wife. I hope you'll join us for a *nosh*. I just baked these cookies to take to the *shul* (synagogue); they're kosher for Passover." This lovely Christian gal, who offered to feed us scrumptious Passover goodies, was a-okay on our list. We thanked Mary and she left through the study door to return to their house.

"Thanks, honey. I love you. See you later," said Rabbi Moses.

He then continued to tell us of his various health maladies, especially about how his herniated disc will sooner or later require back surgery. We talked about the shitty state of health insurance and then the conversation led to medicinal marijuana. Since it was legal in New Jersey, Moses had somehow been able to get a prescription. I had whispered to Solly when we first walked in, "This place smells like pot," but he shushed me. Solly just thought it was the rabbi's cigar.

Then Moses whipped out a joint and asked us, "Do you mind?" Not only were we stunned—we were delightfully surprised when he asked us if we'd like a toke.

Well, Solly and I hired him on the spot! I then appointed Solly as our designated driver of the day and I took a few nice, long hits of the green stuff, courtesy of the State of New Jersey and Holy Moses.

As I began to mellow out (which Solly will tell you requires a lot of work due to my intense personality—this had to be some very potent weed), Solly filled Moses in on the venue, the time and date, and even wrote a check for the deposit. By that time, I couldn't even write my name.

Of course, since it's been known that those who partake of the pot will get food cravings, Rabbi Moses brought up the topic of Jewish chicken soup. He claimed that although his mom was fucked in the brain, memories of her chicken soup made him smile. "Mary tries really hard to make a good chicken soup, but it's just not like my manic mom's," he said.

"Just you wait until you try *Jane Goldman's Jewish Penicillin*," I managed to blurt out while still hazed on my high. "I promise to get you some on or before our wedding ceremony." Shit, by then I was having such a case of the munchies that even I, who didn't eat chicken, would have eaten that soup.

"That's a deal," said Rabbi Moses.

We said our goodbyes as I blew a kiss to the rabbi—I told you I was mellow—and Solly led me to the car where I began to laugh hysterically. Who knew the Virgin Mary of Church Street would be home to a rabbi and his *shikse* wife?

Here we are, friends and family, together assembled for our long-awaited wedding. I was worried it would rain because every day for the past fifty-nine years it did, or so Jane Goldman used to remind me until I was old enough to expect this on my own. It always rained on my birthday. But the sun is shining and it's a mild seventy degrees by noon.

Our wedding day, November 2, would also be my sixtieth birthday. Solly joked that from now on he'd only have to remember one day for two occasions.

We reserved a block of hotel rooms for guests coming from afar. Of course, we had rooms for our immediate families all on one floor for convenience. A few months before, we had interviewed the party planner at the Holiday Inn in Hasbrouck Heights, New Jersey, after we had attended an eightieth birthday party brunch and fell in love with the sky-lit ballroom and the high quality of delectable cuisine. When Solly and I walked into that room for the birthday party, we both said in unison, "This is it!"

The morning of November 2, I sent Solly, already dressed in his fancy gray suit and boutonniere, along with Lori's fiancé Paul, out to Dunkin' Donuts for coffee while the makeup artist applied finishing touches to both Lori's and my *punims*. Lori and Paul recently became engaged after dating for eight—yes, eight—years, so she would now have a chance to show everyone the nice rock on her left ring finger at her mama's wedding.

Lori wore a purple sleeveless sheath that accentuated her size-four figure and silver strappy sandals.

Mitchell and Josh, already engaged to be married, were responsible for keeping everyone out of our room while we got dressed and, in general, just directing those on our room block floor away from sneaking a peek at the bridal dressing room.

Esther-Chanah and my sweet Leah-Shira would be arriving momentarily by limo directly from the airport. They took the red-eye from San Francisco, so with the time difference I was hoping Leah-Shira slept on the plane eastbound. I had sent a lavender dress for *Zeeseleh* to San Francisco a few weeks earlier in little girls' size six like Esti advised. Esti had explained to Leah-Shira that *Bubbe* Fanny and *Zaidey* (Grandpa) Solly were having a wedding in New Jersey, so they'd have to fly to New Jersey in an airplane again for our big party. I had a petite lavender bouquet made for my *Zeeseleh*, and a lavender wrist corsage made for Esti.

Lori helped me into my purple jersey gown and cape with silver sequins along the v-neckline. I had silver-sequined flip-flops, of course, and silver blingy jewelry. The night before, Solly gave me a silver and diamond heart necklace for my birthday and I made sure to wear that around my neck as "something new.. Something old, something new, as the saying goes. Well, I was old, so that took care of that.

Esti and Leah-Shira arrived along with Solly, who brought me a Dunkin' Donuts dark roast and a humongous chocolate chip muffin. "*Bubbe*, you look so pretty," said *Zeeseleh* as I grabbed her and her mommy for a bear hug. "Mommy said to tell you I slept on the plane so you wouldn't worry." *Oy*, even Esti knew me already.

I offered to share my muffin which Esti and Leah-Shira gladly accepted.

I told them there would be a phenomenal brunch soon after the ceremony that would include salads, pasta, salmon, French toast, scrambled eggs, and a carving station with corned beef and pastrami. Leah-Shira's eyes lit up when she heard corned beef. "I love corned beef and brisket, *Bubbe* Fanny!" Whose grandchild is this, after all?

Leah-Shirah went to the fridge to look for some juice and asked, "What's in that jar, *Bubbe*? It looks like *pishy* (short for urine in Yiddish)!" We all laughed. I told her that it was chicken soup I made for the rabbi. I said that I called it *Jane Goldman's Jewish Penicillin* and that I would tell her all about her great-grandma one day soon. She smiled.

Lori's fiancé, Paul, and Mitchell and his fiancé, Josh, all wore gray pinstripe suits with white shirts and lavender ties. I made sure they each had lavender boutonnieres as well.

Solly donned his purple *kippah* with silver stars, then he kissed my cheek. Then he said, "Let's do this, *mameleh*!"

"Wait, don't forget the rabbi's chicken soup," I said. That would be far better than any monetary tip we could give him. Josh grabbed the jar from our mini-fridge and we left the hotel room and headed, en masse, to the elevator.

At 12:30 promptly, we all entered the Americana Ballroom as our favorite band, Hemp, played hippie music from the seventies. As we walked from the entranceway to the sky-lit stage where Rabbi Moses was waiting by the white, silver, and lavender lace *chuppah*, we greeted many of our guests. I saw Mandiyee, Myrna, and Bobby—who said that Freddy was doing well in rehab—and Duni-B and Puff, who both still had their heads buried in their phones.

A large framed photo of Solly's mom, Mindy Rabinowitz, who had passed away five weeks before our wedding day just short of her ninety-second birthday, held a ceremonial seat of honor on a regal gold velvet chair to the right of the *chuppah*, along with her corsage, which framed her photo.

We met briefly with Rabbi Moses at a table set up for the signing of our *ketubah* (Jewish marriage license). I told him that Josh brought in a quart jar of

Jane Goldman's Jewish Penicillin but I didn't know where it was. He assured me he wouldn't leave without it.

"I now pronounce you husband and wife," said Rabbi Moses, as teary-eyed Solly kissed his teary-eyed Fanny. You could tell Solly was nervous when instead stomping on the *mazel tov* glass, he stomped on the glass jar of chicken soup. We jumped aside as shards of glass and yellow liquid splashed all around the *chuppah*. Well, at least we found it. "Josh!"

Leah-Shira ran to her mommy and said, "Now it really looks like *pishy* on the floor!"

The entire room of a hundred-some-odd guests shouted in unison, "*Mazel tov!*" as many who were seated close to the *chuppah* backed away from the glistening liquid. Hemp began to play James Taylor's "How Sweet It Is" as the wait staff rushed in with a mop to clean up the fragrant, wasted mess.

Rabbi Moses laughed and said, "It's still a *mazel tov*-broken glass, but you owe me a jar of chicken soup." After all, the tradition is to break a glass at a Jewish wedding. To my knowledge, there is no law as to the size or type of glass that is broken.

"I guess we'll have to invite you for dinner, Rabbi," was all I could say as I asked him to join us for the brunch. He gladly accepted and found a seat next to our friends from Geneseo, New York.

We managed to grab a few mouthfuls of the delicious brunch goodies and then walked around to speak with our guests. My old Bronx home girls, Sara Ornstein and Cami Arena, were seated at the same table. I was thrilled to see my lifelong friends together again. They hadn't seen each other in nearly forty years. And Milagros sat with them. She came with her son and daughter-in-law because at eighty she was no longer driving.

Hemp, with its talented *goyishe* musicians, did us the honor of learning "Hava Nagila" just for our wedding. And in that ballroom, all those who were able-bodied joined in surely one of the largest *hora* (a high-spirited Israeli-Jewish circle dance, often accompanied by the song "Hava Nagila") dance circles that the

Americana Ballroom has ever witnessed.

"*L'chaim!*" said our guests, in unison, as Solly led a toast with the all-you-can-drink mimosas.

twenty-nine

Boy Marries Goy

Today's book tour stop takes us to the Bustleton section of Northeast Philadelphia. Miltie Lipschitz, owner of the Lipschitz Green Grocer chain of farmers' markets and health food stores throughout Pennsylvania, is a cousin of Bobby's. While Bobby says that Miltie is a nervous type and tends to stutter under pressure, she thought we could do a segment featuring a colorful salad using many of his organic goodies.

"Organic?" I asked Bobby. "Who gives a shit about organic? You're gonna die anyway!"

"Just do it," said Bobby. "Maybe it'll sell more of your books and boost our ratings in Pennsylvania."

"Yes, boss," I said. "But it didn't seem to help Freddy even though Tina's been feeding him that organic crap for years."

"Point taken," said Bobby. "But he's actually coming along nicely. I expect to hear from Tina soon, so I'll keep you posted."

Our limo drops us off at the corporate headquarters of Lipschitz Green Grocer and we are escorted to a roomy studio where they usually do demos for supermarket chains who carry their products. There is a small audience of locals. Our backdrop is set up with assorted fresh fruits and veggies in all the colors of

223

the prism.

"Wow, you have quite a rainbow assortment of fruits and veggies; it looks like a Gay Pride flag in here. What are we making today?" I ask Miltie as he shakes my hand.

"Hhhhow ddddoes bbbbaby sssspinach wwwith chchchick pppeas and ssssweet llllemon vvvvinaigrette sssssound ttttto yyyyyou?" stutters Miltie.

"Aw, c'mon Miltie, there's no need to be nervous. I don't bite, though Solly might beg to differ," I say as I whisk the honey and olive oil with the fresh lemon juice.

We proceed by placing the baby spinach into a large purple salad bowl and then add the drained chick peas. After the dressing is well-whisked, Miltie drizzles it over the large salad already in the bowl. I add a pinch of salt and pepper and mix it around with tongs. His assistants pass around plastic bowls with forks to the hungry audience.

"Hey Miltie," I was compelled to say. "If you're Lipschitz, my ass whistles." The audience laughs. "Sorry, I couldn't resist, but I bet you heard that a lot growing up."

"Aaactually, nnnnooo, I ddddidn't," he says. I guess it must be a Bronx thing because Solly told me afterwards that he'd never heard that before in New Jersey either. I thought it was kind of cute, though, myself. Growing up in the Bronx, we used to tease unfortunate kids who had the then-common Lipschitz moniker.

"But seriously, Miltie, you've really got to change that name. Who would bless a kid with the name 'Lipschitz'?" I asked hypothetically.

I continued, "All this colorful, healthy stuff here reminds me of what I did with the Carmen Miranda fruit hat from a huge Bette Midler ice sculpture at my son Mitch's wedding in this great state of Pennsylvania."

My baby boy's getting married today! You won't believe how much work we had to do to turn around a wedding in only two weeks. But Mitchell and Josh had the time off, Mitchell from his doctoral studies and Josh from his IT job. And they were in New Jersey anyway for Solly's and my wedding. We let the boys do their magic and you won't believe what an amazing job they did.

So here we go again, and soon it will be Lori's and Paul's turn.

It was one big, happy Feinman-Goldman-Eldred-Rabinowitz-Leiberman family here at the chic Deux Couilles Golf Club on the Main Line in Philadelphia. Gay marriage has been legal for some time now throughout this great USA. The boys' wonderful justice of the peace, Sybil Manners, made sure to remind everyone just as she pronounced them husband and husband to thunderous cheers from the guests.

The groom's maids on Josh's side all wore kelly green to match his bowtie. Lori, as Mitchell's groom's maid of honor and his groom's maids, including Esther-Chanah, all wore royal blue like his bowtie. Leah-Shira and Josh's niece, Annie, were picture-perfect flower girls in matching green and blue party dresses.

Mazel tovs were cheerfully exchanged as Mitchell stomped on a glass, this time wrapped in a white napkin. They weren't going to take any chances of stepping on anything else like Solly did at our wedding. But although it started out a warm autumn day, by then it was pouring a cold, windy rain and the outdoor canvas canopy collapsed on everyone, flooding the entire terrace just as husband kissed husband.

Everyone made a mad dash for the cocktail hour which was, luckily, held indoors. Sopping guests dried off with white terry-cloth pool towels. Robin Hood-costumed gorgeous male waiters showing well-sculpted thighs in green tights served up shrimp, spring rolls, and wings on bountiful large silver trays. Now was the time for me to run to the potty before dinner was served and the toasts began. Boy, was I glad I didn't wait.

I watched the scared servers dealing with hungry Jews and Gentiles who downed the hors d'oeuvres like lions attacking their prey. I walked past the ballroom where the reception was to be held. There I noticed, smack in the center of the ballroom, a life-sized ice sculpture of Bette Midler dressed as Carmen Miranda, complete with a delicately-carved fruit hat. In front of Icy Bette was an only slightly smaller upright chopped liver mold of the happy couple, husband and husband. While no one was looking, I quickly entered the ballroom and added a little artwork of my own. Solly has always said that I'm great with my hands.

An hour later, wedding planner and master of ceremonies Mariah Curry, decked out in drag and hired by Mitchell and Josh for his strong resemblance to the gay cult idol of a similar name, began to introduce the newlyweds as the guests piled into the Merry Maidens Ballroom. With the DJ playing music in the background, Mariah presented the happy couple and began his karaoke version of their wedding song, "Dream Lover."

Suddenly, shrieks, then laughter began to reverberate from the crowd in the cavernous cathedral-ceilinged room. Mostly *oy veys*, especially from ninety-five-year-old *Tante* Bella and the various *alter yentas* (old lady gossipers) strolling by with their walkers who hobbled, as quickly as they could, to their seats. I watched like a peeping Tom as they began fanning themselves with their Lady Gaga paper fan party favors, hoping to avoid fainting.

Apparently, someone—who might that be?—swiped two very stiff ice bananas from Bette Midler-Carmen Miranda's fruit hat and placed them in their anatomically correct location on the two grooms' chopped liver mold.

As we all enjoyed our dinners, I saw SpaceCowboy/Joe trying to extinguish the ire of his lactose-intolerant "vegamarian" missus who was fuming about the cream sauce on her pasta. Suddenly, Rona Feinman grabbed a plate destined for another guest off of Robin Hood's silver tray and proceeded to scarf down a blood-rare king cut of prime rib. I wonder what it is about beef that puts that orgasmic look on many a Jewish woman's *punim*?

I ran up to Mariah Curry, quickly asked to borrow his microphone, and toasted the happy couple. "Here's to my little boy Mitchell and his *sheyna* (handsome, pretty) husband, Josh. Everyone, *ess gezunta hayt* (eat in good health)."

epilogue

So, Solly and I finally got to take a honeymoon in Florida and the Keys arranged by Myrna and Bobby as a wedding gift.

"Thanks, ladies," I said.

"There's a catch," said Myrna. "We'd like you to do just one demo in Boca Raton while you're down there."

For me, doing anything in Boca isn't a hardship because it's my most favorite place on earth. It's a Jewish girl's paradise where I can see palm trees and wear my beloved flip-flops even in dead of winter, unlike up north in freakin' New Jersey. Hell, there are Toojay's Delis all over the state. And, the Festival Flea Market is just down the road from Boca in Pompano Beach. What could be bad?

"Deal," I said as I hugged my bosses.

So a week later, a Florida affiliate station's crew was setting up and we'd be demoing *Solly's Super-sensational Brownies* for a group of *really* old seniors at Warbling Woods, a large, sprawling retirement community off of Yamato Road in Boca. Solly's my good luck charm and is seated in the audience. He's probably the youngest man in the room, not including the stage hands. The average age of the audience appears to be about ninety. I just hope they stay awake to sample the brownies.

"So, youngsters (flattery will get you everywhere), my new husband Solly's recipe is amazing: double the chocolate, double the butter, double the eggs—you get the picture. And the pièce de résistance is the secret ingredient: espresso powder." While I poured the mixed ingredients into a baking pan lined with parchment paper and waited for the stagehands to swap with previously baked and cooled brownies, I decided to take questions.

A hand went up on the side of the room toward the back. "So, Fanny, what about the whipped cream and cherries like at the Mamaroneck Motel?" I had to grab a handkerchief as I started to tear up. It was Freddy Giordano, seated beside his Tina, and he looked pretty damned fetching. I ran to both of them and grabbed them for a group hug only to see that Freddy had to stand up with a cane as the stroke had left him partially paralyzed.

Meanwhile, the stagehands were passing out brownie samples to the audience. I continued to take questions while everyone enjoyed Solly's delicious treats. For some reason, there seemed to be a mellow vibe spreading throughout the audience.

Another hand went up in the back. What a surprise! It was none other than my friend, Ellwood Timber, who *schlepped* up from Miami Beach to say hi when Mandiyee told him that Solly and I would be visiting for our honeymoon.

"Can you please ask your people to make the music a bit louder? Or maybe you can just pass out the hearing aid batteries?" I ran again to the back of the room and gave Ellwood a big kiss on the cheek.

"I'd rather have a leather-clad, bearded stud do that and my cheek wouldn't be my first anatomical choice. But you'll do," said Elli with an impish grin. This time, his friend Gary was holding his dog, Woody, in the lobby so I wouldn't sneeze which would have been a dead giveaway that there was a pooch in the room.

They were playing songs from the forties and fifties. Pretty soon, the entire room of elderly started to sway in their chairs and I had a great idea—something I'm sure hadn't been done before and something that the Warbling

Woods' recreation director could use long after I'd returned back home: *chair-twerking for seniors.*

I sat my ass on the stool in front of my cooking station and asked everyone to join me. A snappy "Great Balls of Fire,, a fifties classic by Jerry Lee Lewis, was playing, now louder, as my ancient groupies gyrated their *tuchases* left, right, and back and forth in their seats.

And of course, I never said anything when Ellwood told me afterward that he had spiked the swapped-out brownies with some very potent weed. That was the *real* secret ingredient. "Congratulations on your marriage, *dahlink*," he said with his endearing Brooklyn Jewish accent. "That was my gift to you and Solly."

He also left us an autographed set of the complete works of Ellwood Timber and a personalized sketch of a couple which he autographed, "Love, Ellwood. Woodstock 1969.. The drawing even had a random coffee stain. It seemed as though Ellwood drank coffee even in his sleep, so it was the watermark of a genuine Ellwood Timber.

As for Myrna's and Bobby's gift, they wanted me to see that Freddy was doing fine and that he and Tina were settled down in a beautiful community for a long overdue retirement.

"Hi Gorgeous," I said to Lori as I saw her name light up my phone. "What's up?"

"Mom, sit down…" *Oy*, this can't be good. My kids always call me Fanny unless something major is happening.

"Spill," I said as I complied with my daughter's orders and sat down on the purple velour recliner in my dressing room.

"You're going to be a grandma again." But their wedding is in three months, I thought as I put my hand over my mouth so as to stop what I might have said. And, since when is Fanny old-fashioned, anyway? Literally, a pregnant pause…

"You mean you've decided to try to get pregnant, like right on your wedding night?"

"No, Mom. We won't be waiting. The deed's done," said Gorgeous. OMG! I'm glad Lori had ordered me to sit down.

Think quickly, Fanny. Lori will be five months preggo at her wedding. We'll just have to get her a comfy, loose-fitting dress. *Wow!* I paused and processed, not wanting to get in trouble, which by now you know happens often.

"Hold on." (Let me take a few tokes on my joint.) "Mazel tov!" I said to my amazing daughter. "I bet Paul is thrilled." Then, "Why'd'ya wait so long, anyway?" I couldn't resist. After all, Lori and Paul have been together now for *ten whole years*!

All my dreams have come true.

With so much *nachas* (pleasure; satisfaction) my Leah-Shira has already brought me in such a short time, another little one will be an even further incentive for the new show idea I've been working on. And Mitchell and Josh have their names on an international adoption list, so maybe they'll be next. I'm *kvelling* (bursting with pride)!

I began to outline kid-friendly recipes created by every possible ethnic variety of grannies. Grandpas are welcome as well. The possibilities are endless…

Now I must tell Myrna and Bobby all about *Fanny Granny*. I think it'll be a hit!

THE END

Acknowledgments

There are many people responsible for this book, so I want to be sure to include everyone. Much of Fanny on Fire is a memoir (surprise, surprise!), though I haven't had a cooking show, yet.

-It was quite therapeutic revisiting in my mind with old friends from my past. Yes, there really was a Freddy Giordano, a Boris Perlmutter, and every one of the other suitors I told you about. You can't really make that shit up. But I'll never tell you their real names.

-To Rudy Shur and Anthony Pomes of Square One: thanks for working with me on *Secrets of Successful Inventing*. Also, thanks for introducing me to the late, great Elliot Tiber, Big Daddy of Woodstock, without whom Fanny's friend Ellwood could not have been perceived.

-I'll even thank SpaceCowboy, but he's probably somewhere out there on a galactic voyage, listening to "Rocket Man," reading space digests while conducting geriatric studies. I hope he's happy.

-Thanks to the real David Tobin, a blessed memory, also with a different name.

-Thanks to my two brothers whose names are not Marty and Harry, and their wives who are not Wanda and Karen.

-To the late Jean and Melvin Goldstein, without whom I wouldn't be here to *kvetch*.

-Special thanks to my two greatest treasures, Dori and Max. You rolled your eyes whenever I mentioned *Fanny on Fire*. I bet you thought I would never do this!

-And to my real-life spicy Solly, also known as Ken Robinson, who laughed with me while I wrote at the dining room table for so many years. We did this together, and the third time's a charm.

-With gratitude and appreciation for Rutherford Rankin and Team Michelkin, who, from query, to synopsis, through first fifty, to full manuscript, caught the true message of Fanny on Fire... tolerance, love, and finding absurdity and humor to help cope with the challenges of growing up an outlier.

-To those who aren't specifically included here—you know who you are—I say a hearty THANK YOU. Sara Ornstein (not her real name) recently passed on just before this book was published. Why do the gems often have to suffer? Thanks for all the memories since 1973, including Togi America, Grossinger's, and that singles dance where I dug up Boris Perlmutter.

-My wish is that my story brings levity and hope to those who turn these pages.

About the Author

Edith G. Tolchin, proud mother of Dori and Max, is married to Ken Robinson. They currently live in New Jersey. She has written non-fiction material for many years, including a business-lifestyle column for an upstate New York newspaper, *Orange Magazine*, *Hudson Valley Life*, *WebMD*, *Bottom Line Personal*, and *Entrepreneur*, and she's been a columnist for *Inventors Digest* since 2000. She's the author and editor of *Secrets of Successful Inventing: From Concept to Commerce*, as well as co-author (with Don Debelak and Eric Debelak) of *Sourcing Smarts: Keeping it Simple and SAFE with China Sourcing and Manufacturing*.

As the owner of EGT Global Trading since 1997, she works with inventors to bring their dreams to life.

Edie's thirty-year kitchen obsession has helped her perfect such delights as *Grammy Jane's Jewish Penicillin*, *Latkes to Die For*, and *Brisket with Secret Sauce*. She craves the chaos of crashing dishes, the clean-up calisthenics from pots boiled over, and the challenging of senses with strange odors and tastes, all of which evoke unique Yiddish profanities.

Stay tuned for the further hilarious adventures of Fanny Goldman, her hubby, spicy Solly Rabinowitz, and the colorful outliers who enrich their lives and, hopefully, yours!

Edie loves to hear from you. Contact her at www.fannyonfire.com or www.edietolchin.com. *L'chaim!*

CPSIA information can be obtained
at www.ICGtesting.com
Printed in the USA
BVOW08s1151191017
498137BV00002B/103/P